Acknowledgements:

    To the late GREAT SHIRLEY ANN MATTHEWS, Dear mother of mine, even though you're with the MOST HIGH right now, your spirit, your soul still lives and breathes here on this earth. I know you can hear me and I know you're OK. Please believe...all your struggles,your pain,your challenges that you overcome are not in VAIN! Please continue to live through me.

    To all my Ancestors Ancient and near Ancient,you did not struggle in VAIN! Thank you all for your struggle and perseverance, continue to live through me. You have been Resurrected!

    To my loving father EDWARD JULIUS JONES thank you for making me the KING I AM! Please continue to live through me.

To my Immediate brothers and sisters UNLIMITED BOUNDS family thank you all, either past or present for your contributions to my life it's definitely not in VAIN! Continue to live through me!

T.O.C

1. A brief history lesson on Natural Law, Commercial Law, Divine Law, Eternal Law, Human Law
a) History into the African diaspora

2. Unity Vow
a) History of the Current Economic System and the hidden secret behind it

3. Esoteric Knowledge
a) Governmental breakdown of it

My goal for putting this book together is to provoke thought. What do I mean by provoking thought? Lets define provoke-to call forth (a feeling, an action etc.) to stir up purposely.

Getting everyone reading this dialogue to start thinking outside the box and doing things differently Whatever! That may be. There is nothing too big,or too small as far as ideas, business

ventures,inventions,creations whether esoterically or physically. We all have that creator spark in us as well as destiny or purpose built into us,because of the powers at be who govern but don't have INHERENTLY AUTHORITY! over the globe the earth is backwards spinning on the same energy with no light to balance the darkness. The reason for always darkness another word for darkness is chaos,confusion,disorientation sprawling down cycle just to name a few. The powers that govern this world want to make every living soul a physical slave. Enslavement of the mind which is esoterically because the motto is whomever controls the mind controls the body. Now stay with me, your mind is an energy center. It's esoteric, meaning we cannot see with our physical eyes a mind. The brain is the storage center and is physical. PLEASE KIM! The mind works esoterically(In the spiritual realm). Duality is a Mindset, lets define mindset-is a set of beliefs that shape how you make sense of the world and yourself. It influences how you think, feel and behave in any given situation. In other words it's PROGRAMING! KIM-keep in mind- LOL whomever controls the mind controls the body. So! If I told you that you're the heir or heiress to an Inheritance WOULD YOU BELIEVE ME!
Option 1 YES if you choose to answer yes then you mindset is entacked and would love to cultivate your mindset to bring out your purpose and or destiny.

Option 2 NO If you choose NO! You don't believe me it's fine NO JUDGMENT here just ask you to please pay attention going forward so you can awaken to your mindset that already exists inside of you laying dormant because it doesn't fit this world system. Let's define a system-A group of interacting or interrelated elements that can act according to a set of rules to form a United! Whole. A system surrounded and influenced by its environment, is described by its boundaries, structure and purpose and expressed in its functioning.

> *They show that the requirements of the law are written on their hearts, their consciences also bearing witness, and their thoughts sometimes accusing them and at other times even defending them.*
>
> *Grace does not destroy nature but perfects it.*

Natural law

Introduction to Aquinas

Thomas Aquinas was an intellectual and religious revolutionary, living at a time of great philosophical, theological and scientific development. He was a member of the Dominican Friars, which at that time was considered to be a cult, and was taught by one of the greatest intellects of the age, **Albert the Great**. In a nutshell Aquinas wanted to move away from Plato's thinking, which was hugely influential at the time, and instead introduce Aristotelian ideas to science, nature and theology.

Aquinas wrote an *incredible* amount — in fact one of the miracles accredited to him was the amount he wrote! His most famous work is *Summa Theologica* and this runs to some three and half thousand pages and contains many fascinating and profound insights, such as proofs for God's existence. The book remained a fundamental basis for Catholic thinking right up to the 1960s! But do not worry we will only be focusing on a few key ideas!

Motivating Natural Law Theory: The Euthyphro Dilemma and Divine Command Theory

The likely answer from a religious person as to *why* we should not steal, or commit adultery is: "because God *forbids* us"; or if we ask *why* we should love our neighbour or give money to charity then the answer is likely to be "because God *commands* it". Drawing this link between what is right and wrong and what God commands and forbids is what is called the *Divine Command Theory* (DCT).

There is a powerful and influential challenge to such an account called the *Euthyphro dilemma* after the challenge was first raised in Plato's *Euthyphro*. The dilemma runs as follows: *Either* God commands something is right because it is, *or* it is right because God commands it. If God commands something because it is right, then God's commands do not make it right, His commands only tell us what is right.

This means God simply drops out of the picture in terms of *explaining why* something is right.

If on the other hand something is right *because* God commands it then *anything* at all could be right; killing children or setting fire to churches could be morally acceptable. But if a moral theory says this then that looks as if the theory is wrong.

Most theists reject the first option and opt for this second option — that God's commands *make* something right. But they then have to face the problem that it makes morality haphazard. This "*arbitrariness problem*" as it is sometimes called, is the reason that many, including Aquinas, give up on the Divine Command Theory.

So for Aquinas what role, if any at all, does God have when it comes to morality? For him, God's commands are there to help us to *come to see* what, as a matter of fact, is right and wrong rather than determine what is right and wrong. That is, Aquinas opts for the first option in the Euthyphro dilemma as stated above. But then this raises the obvious question: if it is not God's commands that make something right and wrong, then what does? Does not God just fall out of the picture? This is where his Natural Law Theory comes in.

Natural Law Theory

Aquinas's Natural Law Theory contains four different types of law: *Eternal Law, Natural Law, Human Law and Divine Law*. The way to understand these four laws and how they relate to one another is via the Eternal Law, so we'd better start there…

By "Eternal Law'" Aquinas means God's rational purpose and plan for *all* things. And because the Eternal Law is part of God's mind then it has always, and will always, exist. The Eternal Law is not simply something that God decided at some point to write.

Aquinas thinks that *everything* has a purpose and follows a plan. He, like Aristotle, is a teleologist (the Greek term "*telos*" refers to what we might call a purpose, goal, end/or the true final function of an object) (not to be confused with a teleological ethical *theory* such as Utilitarianism) and believes that *every* object has a *telos*; the acorn has the *telos* of growing into an oak; the eye a *telos* of seeing; a rat of eating and reproducing etc. If something fulfils its purpose/plan then it is following the Eternal Law.

Aquinas thinks that something is *good as* far as it fulfils its purpose/plan. This fits with common sense. A "*good*" eye is one which sees well, an acorn is a good if it grows into a strong oak tree.

But what about humans? Just as a good eye is to see, and a good acorn is to grow then a good human is to...? Is to what? How are we going to finish this sentence? What do you think?

Aquinas thinks that the answer is *reason* and that it is this that makes us distinct from rats and rocks. What is right for me and you as humans is to act according to reason. If we act according to reason then we are partaking in the *Natural Law*.

If we all act according to reason, then we will all agree to some overarching general rules (what Aquinas calls *primary precepts*). These are *absolute* and binding on all rational agents and because of this Aquinas rejects *relativism*.

The first primary precept is that *good is to be pursued and done and evil avoided.* He thinks that this is the guiding principle for all our decision making.

Before unpacking this, it is worth clarifying something about what "law" means. Imagine that we are playing Cluedo and we are trying to work out the identity of the murderer. There are certain rules about how to move around the board, how to deal out cards, how to reveal the murderer etc. These rules are all written down and can be consulted.

However, in playing the game there are other rules that operate which are so obvious that they are neither written down nor spoken. One such rule is that a claim made in the game cannot both be true and false; if it *is* Professor Plum who is the murderer then it cannot be true that it *is not* Professor Plum who is the murderer. These are *internal rules* which *any* rational person can come to recognize by simply thinking and are not external like the other rules — such as you can only have one guess as to the identity of the murderer. When Aquinas talks of Natural Laws, he means internal rules and not external ones.

Natural Law does not generate an external set of rules that are written down for us to consult but rather it generates general rules that any rational agent can come to recognize simply in virtue of being rational. For example, for Aquinas it is not as if we need to check whether we should pursue good and avoid evil, as it is just part of how we already think about things.

Aquinas gives some more examples of primary precepts:

1. *Protect and preserve human life.*
2. *Reproduce and educate one's offspring.*
3. *Know and worship God.*
4. *Live in a society.*

These precepts are *primary* because they are true for *all people in all instances* and are consistent with Natural Law.

Aquinas also introduces what he calls the *Human Law* which gives rise to what he calls "*Secondary Precepts*". These might include such things as do not drive above 70mph on a motorway, do not kidnap people, always wear a helmet when riding a bike, do not hack into someone's bank account. Secondary precepts are *not generated by our reason* but rather they are imposed by governments, groups, clubs, societies etc.

It is *not* always morally acceptable to follow secondary precepts. It is only morally acceptable *if* they are consistent with the Natural Law. If they are, then we ought to follow them, if they are not, then we ought not. To see why think through an example.

Consider the secondary precept that "*if you are a woman and you live in Saudi Arabia then you are not allowed to drive*". Aquinas would argue that this secondary precept is practically *irrational* because it treats people differently based on an arbitrary difference (gender). He would reason that if the men in power in Saudi actually really thought hard then they too would recognize that this law is morally wrong. This in turn means that Aquinas would think that *this* human law *does not* fit with the Natural Law. Hence, it is morally wrong to follow a law that says that men can, and women cannot, drive. So although it is presented as a secondary precept, because it *is not* in accordance with Natural Law, it is what Aquinas calls an *apparent good*. This is in contrast with those secondary precepts which *are* in accordance with the Natural Law and which he calls the *real goods*.

Unlike primary precepts, Aquinas is *not* committed to there being only one set of secondary precepts for all people in all situations. It is consistent with Aquinas's thinking to have a law to drive on the right in the US and on the left in the UK as there is no practical reason to think that there is one correct side of the road on which to drive.

It is clear that on our own we are not very good at discovering primary precepts and consequently Aquinas thinks that what we ought to do is talk and interact with people. To discover our real goods — our secondary precepts which accord with Natural Law — we need to be part of a society. For example, we might think that "treat Christians as secondary citizens" is a good secondary precept until we talk and live with Christians. The more we can think and talk with others in society the better and it is for this reason that "live in society" is itself a primary precept.

But looking at what we have said already about Natural Laws and primary and secondary precepts, we might think that there is no need for God. If we can learn these primary precepts by rational reflection then God simply drops out of the story (recall the Euthyphro dilemma above).

Just to recap as there are lots of moving parts to the story. We now have Eternal Law (God's plans/purpose for all things), Natural Laws (our partaking in the Eternal Law which leads to primary precepts), Human Laws (humans making specific laws to capture the truths of the Natural Laws which lead to secondary precepts) and now finally Aquinas introduces the *Divine Law*.

The Divine Law, which is discovered through *revelation*, should be thought of as the Divine equivalent of the Human Law (those discovered through rational reflection and created by people). Divine laws are those that God has, in His grace, seen fit to give us and are those "mysteries", those rules given by God which we find in scripture; for example, the ten commandments. But why introduce the Divine Law at all? It certainly feels we have enough Laws. Here is a story to illustrate Aquinas's answer.

A number of years ago I was talking to a minister of a church. He told me about an instance where a married man came to ask his advice about whether to finish an affair he was having. The man's reasoning went as follows — "I am having an affair which just feels so right, we are both very much in love and surely God would want what is best for me! How could it be wrong if we are so happy?"

In response, the minister opened the Bible to the Ten Commandments and pointed out the commandment that it says that it is wrong to commit adultery. Case closed. The point of this story is simple. We can be confused and mistaken about what we think we have most reason to do and because of this we need someone who actually knows the mind of God to guide us, and who better to know this than God Himself. This then is precisely what is revealed in the Divine Law.

Or consider another example. We recognize that we find it hard to forgive our friends and nearly always impossible to forgive our enemies. We tell ourselves we have the right to be angry, to bear grudges, etc. Isn't this just human? However, these human reasons are *distortions* of the Eternal Law. We need some guidance when it comes to forgiveness and it is where the Divine Law which tells us that we should forgive others — including our enemies. Following the Human Laws *and* the Divine Laws will help us to fulfil our purposes and plans and be truly happy.

Summary of Aquinas's Natural Law Theory

For Aquinas everything has a function (a *telos*) and the good thing (s) to do are those acts that fulfil that function. Some things such as acorns, and eyes, just do that naturally. However, humans are free and hence need guidance to find the right path. That right path is found through *reasoning* and generates the "internal" Natural Law. By following the Natural Law we participate in God's purpose for us in the Eternal Law.

However, the primary precepts that derive from the Natural Law are quite general, such as, *pursue good and shun evil*. So we need to create secondary precepts which can actually guide our day-to-day behaviour. But we are fallible so sometimes we get these secondary precepts wrong, sometimes we get them right. When they are wrong they only reflect our apparent goods. When they are right they reflect our real goods.

Finally, however good we are because we are finite and sinful, we can only get so far with rational reflection. We need some *revealed guidance* and this comes in the form of Divine Law. So to return to the Euthyphro dilemma. God's commands through the Divine Law are ways of *illuminating* what is in fact morally acceptable and *not what determines* what is morally acceptable. Aquinas rejects the Divine Command Theory.

Putting this into Practice: The Doctrine of Double Effect (DDE)

Let's consider some examples to show that what we have said so far might actually work. Imagine someone considering suicide. Is this morally acceptable or not? Recall, it is part of the Natural Law to preserve and protect human life. Clearly suicide is not preserving and protecting human life. It is therefore irrational to kill oneself and cannot be part of God's plan for our life; hence it is morally unacceptable.

Imagine that someone is considering having an abortion after becoming pregnant due to rape. The same reasoning is going to apply. We ought to preserve and protect human life and hence an abortion in this case is morally wrong.

However, as we will see, Aquinas thinks that there are *some* instances where it *is* morally acceptable to kill an innocent person and therefore there may be occasions when it is morally acceptable to kill a fœtus. But how can this be correct? Will this not violate the primary precept about preserving life? The answer is to understand that for Aquinas, *an action is not just about what we do externally but is also about what we do internally* (i.e. our motivations). With this distinction he can show that, for example, killing an innocent *can be* morally acceptable.

To make this clear, Aquinas introduces one of his most famous ideas: the "*Doctrine of Double Effect*". Let's see how this works.

Imagine a child brought up in a physically, sexually and emotionally abusive family. He is frequently scared for his life and is locked in the house for days at a time. One day when his father is drunk and ready to abuse him again he quickly grabs a kitchen knife and slashes his father's artery. His father bleeds out and dies in a matter of minutes. Do you think the son did anything wrong?

Many people would say that he did nothing morally wrong and in fact, some might even go as far as to say that he should get a pat on the back for his actions. What about Aquinas? What would he say?

We might think that given the Natural Law to "preserve and protect life" he would say that this action is morally wrong. But, in fact, he would say the son's action was not morally wrong.

So why is the son killing the father not in direct contradiction with the primary precept? Aquinas asks us to consider the difference between the external act — the fact that the father was killed, and the internal act — the motive.

In our example, the action is one of *self-defence* because of the son's internal action and because of

this, Aquinas would think the killing is morally acceptable. This distinction and conclusion is possible because of Aquinas's Doctrine of Double Effect which states that if an act fulfils four conditions then it is morally acceptable. If not, then it is not.
1. The first principle is that the act must be a *good* one.
2. The second principle is that the act must come about before the consequences.
3. The third is that the intention must be good.
4. The fourth, it must be for serious reasons.

This is abstract so let's go back to our example. The act of the son was performed to *save his own life* so that is good — we can tick (1). Moreover, the act to save his life came about first — we can tick (2). The son did not first act to kill his father in order to save his own life. That would be doing evil to bring about good and that is never morally acceptable. The intention of the son was to preserve and protect his life, so the intention was good — tick (3). Finally, the reasons were serious as it was his life or his father's life — tick (4).

So given that the act meets all four principles, it is in line with the DDE and hence the action is *morally acceptable*, even though it caused someone to die and hence seems contrary to the primary precept of preserving life.

We can draw a contrasting case. Imagine that instead of slashing his father in self-defence, the son *plans* the killing. He works out the best time, the best day and then sets up a tripwire causing his father to fall from his flat window to his death. Does this action meet the four criteria of the DDE? Well, no, because the son's *intention is to kill the father rather than save his own life* — we must put a cross at (3).

We have already seen that suicide is morally impermissible for Aquinas, so does that mean that *any* action you take that leads knowingly to your own death is morally wrong? No. Because even though the external act of your own death is the same, the internal act — the intention — might be different. *An action is judged via the Natural Law both externally and internally.*

Imagine a case where a soldier sees a grenade thrown into her barracks. Knowing that she does not have time to defuse it or throw it away, she throws herself on the grenade. It blows up, killing her but saving other soldiers in her barracks. Is this wrong or right? Aquinas says this is morally acceptable given DDE. If we judge this act *both* internally and externally we'll see why.

The intention — the internal act — was *not* to kill herself even though she could *foresee* that this was certainly what was going to happen. The act itself is good, to save her fellow soldiers (1). The order is right, she is not doing evil so good will happen (2). The intention is good, it is to save her fellow soldiers (3). The reason is serious, it concerns people's lives (4).

Contrast this with a soldier who decides to kill herself by blowing herself up. The intention is not good and hence the DDE does *not* permit this suicidal action.

Finally, imagine that a woman is pregnant and also has inoperable uterine cancer. The doctors have two choices; to take out the uterus and save the mother, but the fœtus will die; or leave the fœtus to develop and be born healthy, but the woman will die. What would Aquinas say in this instance? Well using the DDE he would say that it is morally *acceptable* to remove the cancer.

The action is to remove the cancer; it has the foreseeable consequences of the fœtus dying but that is not what is intended. The action — to remove the cancer — is good (1). The act of removing the cancer comes before the death of the fœtus (2). The intention to save the woman's life is also good (3). Finally, the reasons are serious as they are about the life and death of the woman and the fœtus (4).

So even though this is a case where the doctor's actions bring about the death of the fœtus it would be acceptable for Aquinas through his Natural Law Theory, as is shown via the DDE.

Some Thoughts about Natural Law Theory

There are many things we might consider when thinking through Aquinas's Natural Law Theory. There are some obvious problems we could raise, such as the problem about whether or not God exists. If God does not exist then the Eternal Law does not exist and therefore the whole theory comes tumbling down. However, as good philosophers we ought always to operate with a *principle of charity* and grant our opponent is rational and give the strongest possible interpretation of their argument. So, let's assume *for the sake of argument* that God exists. How plausible is Aquinas's theory? There are a number of things that we can pick up on.

Aquinas's theory works on the idea that if something is "natural", that is, if it fulfils its function, then it is morally acceptable, but there are a number of unanswered questions relating to "*natural*".

We might ask, why does "natural" matter? We can think of things that are not "natural" but which are perfectly acceptable, and things which *are* natural which are not. For example, wearing clothes, taking medication and body piercing certainly are not natural, but we would not want to say such things are morally wrong.

On the other hand we might consider that violence *is* a natural response to an unfaithful partner, but also think that such violence is morally unacceptable. So it is not true that we can discover what is morally acceptable or not simply by discovering what is natural and what is not.

Put this worry aside. Recall, Aquinas thinks that reproduction is natural and hence reproduction is morally acceptable. This means that sex that *does not* lead to reproduction is morally unacceptable. Notice that Aquinas is not saying that if sex does not lead to pregnancy it is wrong. After all, sometimes the timing is not right. His claim is rather that if there is *no potential* for sex to lead to pregnancy then it is wrong. However, even with this qualification this would mean a whole host of things such as homosexuality and contraception are morally wrong. We might take this as a reason to rethink Aquinas's moral framework (we discuss these apparent problems in more detail in Chapter 10).

There is, though, a more fundamental worry at the heart of this approach (and Aristotle's) to ethics. Namely, they think that *everything* has a goal (*telos*). Now, with some things this might be plausible. Things such as the eye or an acorn have a clear function — to grow, to see — but what about humans? This seems a bit less obvious! Do humans (rather than our individual parts) really have a *telos*? There are certainly some philosophers — such as the existentialists, for example **Simone de Beauvoir** (1908–1986) — who think that there is no such thing as human nature and no such thing as a human function or goal. But if we are unconvinced that humans have a goal, then this whole approach to ethics seems flawed.

Next we might raise questions about DDE. Go back to our example about abortion. For Aquinas it *is* morally acceptable to remove the uterus even if we know that in doing so the fœtus will die. What is not morally acceptable is to intend to kill the fœtus by removing the uterus. On first reading this seems to make sense; we have an intuitive feel for what DDE is getting at. However, when we consider it in more detail it is far from clear.

Imagine two doctors who (apparently) do exactly the same thing, they both remove the uterus and the fœtus dies. The one intends to take out the uterus — in full knowledge that the fœtus will die — the other intends to kill the fœtus. For the DDE to work in the way that Aquinas understands it, this difference in intention makes the moral difference between the two doctors. However, is there really a moral difference? To put pressure on the answer that there is, ask yourself what you think it means to intend to do something. If the first doctor says "I did not intend to kill the fœtus" can we make sense of this? After all, if you asked her "did you know that in taking out the uterus the fœtus would die?" she would say "yes, of course". But if she did this and the fœtus died, did not she intend (in some sense) to kill the fœtus? So this issue raises some complex questions about the nature of the mind, and how we might understand intentions.

Finally, we might wonder how easy it is to work out what actually to do using the Natural Law. We would hope our moral theory gives us direction in living our lives. That, we might think, is precisely the role of a moral theory. But how might it work in this case?

For Aquinas, if we rationally reflect then we arrive at the right way of proceeding. If this is in line with the Natural Law and the Divine Law then it is morally acceptable. If it is out of line, then it is not. The assumption is that the more we think, the more rational we become, the more convergence there will be. We'll all start to have similar views on what is right and wrong. But is this too optimistic? Very often, even after extensive reflection and cool deliberation with friends and colleagues, it is not obvious to us what we as rational agents should do. We all know people we take to be rational, but we disagree with them on moral issues. And even in obviously rational areas such as mathematics, the best mathematicians are not able to agree. We might then be sceptical that as rational agents we will come to be in line with the Natural and Divine Laws.

Aquinas is an intellectual giant. He wrote an incredible amount covering a vast array of topics. His influence has been immense. His central idea is that humans are created by God to reason — that is our function. Humans do the morally right thing if we act in accordance with reason, and the morally wrong thing if we don't.
Aquinas is an incredibly subtle and complex thinker. For example, his Doctrine of Double Effect makes us reflect on

what we actually mean by "actions", "intentions" and "consequences". His work remains much discussed and researched and typically still plays a central role in a Christian Ethics that rejects Divine Command Theory

Common Law
COMMON LAW *and the* LAW OF REASON

James R Stoner Jr.

Like cousins who resemble one another, common law and natural law are sometimes confused. Both are unwritten law; both claim to be anchored in reason and to discern principles of right and wrong; both have been invoked by judges to confine (if not simply void) acts of positive legislation, and derided by others who oppose such action. There is in fact a deep affinity between common law and natural law, but it is better at the outset to describe their differences, and best to do this historically. Indeed, starting from the past rather than from nature is already a characteristic means of distinguishing common law from natural law.

Common law is first and foremost the customary law of England, as applied in the courts of law. In its classic era (the seventeenth century) and in its classic text at the time of the American Founding (Blackstone's *Commentaries on the Laws of England*), the common law was said to exist "from time immemorial," that is, so long that "the memory of man runneth not to the contrary." Historical research eventually showed that most of its rules and rights had an origin in time; for a while it was settled that a custom would be accepted as valid if it were in place in 1189, at the end of the reign of Henry II, whose reform of the royal courts established the framework for administering justice in England that was to remain in place until the late 19th century. As written records came to be made of the decisions of the royal courts, judicial precedents, seen as the most authoritative evidence of a custom, were held to have the force of law: not because judges willfully made law, but because of the principle of natural justice that similar cases ought to be similarly decided.

Common law judges decide cases on the basis of the specific facts in light of all applicable law. Actually, the determination of the facts is characteristically by a jury, traditionally "twelve good men and true," who issue a verdict upon a unanimous vote, following instructions of the judge as to the law that governs the case. Due process, in a criminal trial, requires a formal accusation, the right of the defendant to call witnesses and not to be forced to be a witness against himself, the right to a jury trial and even the right to play a role in the choice of his jurors, the presumption of innocence until proven guilty "beyond a reasonable doubt," and more. Before a trial, the accused is ordinarily entitled to be released on bail and in general to have the privilege of the writ of habeas corpus, guaranteeing that there be no imprisonment without a trial. After a trial, he cannot be tried again for the same offense nor punished in any way except as specified by law, and he has, besides, a right to appeal his verdict. In civil trials at common law, many of these rules are altered, because both parties are equal before the law and either might have initiated proceedings in a dispute. The standard of judgment in civil trials is preponderance of the evidence, and the judgment typically awards monetary damages. Juries were traditionally involved in civil cases as well as criminal ones, though they are increasingly less common in the former. Still, the right to appeal remains intact, and even more than in criminal cases, where crimes are now defined by code rather than by precedent, similar civil cases typically establish the parameters for decision in subsequent cases, unless there is in the circumstances something genuinely new.

There is much about common-law due process that is not strictly speaking a requirement of natural law: no one today would say that justice is impossible anywhere a jury is not composed of twelve, or if its verdicts are not unanimous, or even if some facts are found by a judge or a panel of judges rather than by a lay jury, and so on. Nevertheless, in at least three ways natural law seems particularly evident in common-law thinking. First, while from the point of view of natural-law theory, common-law due process is one among many "determinations" a society might choose in establishing a system of justice, by settling on a particular and stable legal process, the common law forms a felicitous package that minimizes the role of political power and maximizes the role of both individual liberty and community assent in the administration of justice, thus serving the demands of the natural law. For instance, though due process does not ensure that courts exert, in Alexander Hamilton's phrase, "neither force nor will, but merely judgment," the various checks and balances built into common-law formalities—from the distinction between judge and jury, to the adversarial nature of proceedings, to the right of appeal—have seemed to its proponents to make it more likely. Moreover, the centrality of the jury at common law suggests deference to common sense at the center of the system and thus constitutes a restraint on elite theorizing and on partisan will.

A second natural-law moment in common law appears in the process of reasoning by appellate courts. In most legal disputes that are appealed, both sides can argue precedents in their favor; the issue is which set of precedents forms the better analogy to the pattern of facts in the case at hand. For example, is an exchange of instant messages more like a phone conversation, which sometimes cannot alter a written contract, or is it like an exchange of written documents, which can? Is a motor home more like a house, and thus entitled to constitutional protection from warrantless searches, or more like a motor vehicle, searchable upon reasonable suspicion? It is no accident that these examples involve technological change, for that seems to be a common source of genuinely new cases. Where, by contrast, the issue suggests a reinterpretation of established precedent, the common law presumes in favor of the tried and true over innovation. Natural law, though in principle anchored in immutable human nature, does not forbid all change in positive law and may even command it: for a law to remain just when the circumstances in which it arose are altered, the law itself might have to change. The ability of common law to develop in the light of reason as a series of precedents unfolds has led scholars to allude to the "open texture of law" in such a system. Its unwrittenness allows judges to adjust the law without exerting raw power, while the formal process of judging—hearing arguments from both sides, focusing on a precise issue in dispute, settling only the case at hand and thus effectively changing the law only as the new rule becomes widely respected and adopted—ought to dampen the arbitrariness of such adjustments.

The third natural law moment in common-law judging appears in the adage that "nothing that is against reason can be lawful," even while the presumption in the common law is for the tried and true. The basic idea is that the law will brook no contradiction within itself, not that judges need be set up as philosopher-kings to ensure the rule of abstract reason; common law judges try first to reconcile apparent contradictions and accommodate all the various sources of law that apply to a particular case. Nevertheless, since at least Sir Edward Coke's opinion in <u>Doctor Bonham's Case</u> (1610), it has been argued that "when an act of parliament is against common right and reason, or repugnant, or impossible to be performed, the common law will control it, and adjudge such act to be void." English practice eventually held that parliamentary sovereignty overrode the claim of reasonableness, but in America this idea helped to birth the practice of judicial review: the power of courts to strike down statutes or executive actions that contradict written constitutions. American courts invoke a written constitution text rather than abstract "reasonableness," but the rule that unconstitutional acts can be voided by courts is itself not written in any constitution. In Alexander Hamilton's words, the principle relies upon "the nature and reason of the thing," or in the words of John Marshall in Marbury v. Madison, on the "theory…essentially attached to a written constitution." Like natural law itself, the common law maxim that "nothing that is against reason can be lawful" is hardly adequate to generate a whole jurisprudence on its own, but it serves case by case to weed contradictions out of the law and thus to make the law a reasonable whole.

Part of the reasonableness of common law is that its judges traditionally did not see their jurisdiction as unlimited; on the contrary, judges can rule only in cases properly presented before them, and the remedies they can impose for the injustices they find are likewise defined and limited by law. In England and in some of the states, separate courts of equity were established for special circumstances where the operation of strict law was thought to work an injustice; in federal law, the same judges were made responsible for law and equity, but until the 1930s the process for filing a case at law and that for moving a bill of equity were entirely distinct. Moreover, although common law courts are courts of general jurisdiction, they have usually co-existed with other specialty courts responsible for distinct areas of law (such as admiralty or martial law). In England, where there is an established church, ecclesiastical courts were likewise separate, while the American tradition of religious liberty allows ecclesiastical law to operate within denominations without state interference, provided civil law itself is not breached. Constitutional law was always more closely entangled with common law. The unwrittenness of the British constitution might be attributed to England's common law tradition, and the American choice for written constitutions might be construed as a rejection of common-law constitutionalism. But the Americans also inherited from the British the tradition of declaring constitutional principles in writing—a tradition that extended back at least to <u>Magna Carta</u> and forward to the <u>English Bill of Rights</u>—and not a few provisions of the latter appear in almost unaltered form in the early American constitutions and in the Bill of Rights that figures so prominently in American constitutional law today.

In discussing common law in relation to natural law, more has been said about the common-law process than about substantive rules of law, many of which—for example, the law of coverture in marriage, or various tenures for the holding of real property—have been radically changed, often by legislation. American judges never held the common law to have been imported intact, but rather only insofar as applicable to American circumstances and as unaltered by local legislation. The English themselves, as long ago as the 17th century, used the analogy of the Argo—the ship of the ancient hero Jason whose planks were replaced one by one while at sea—to explain how the common law can remain constant even as its particular rules are altered to adapt to changing circumstances.More impressed by the change than the continuity, legal theorists in the 20th century began to refer to common law as "judge-made law," and they were led in this reinterpretation by Oliver Wendell Holmes, Jr., who also belittled natural law as the drunken dream of the self-deluded. To refute Holmes's interpretation would go beyond the bounds of this article, but it is perhaps enough to note the link between his redefinition of common law as purely positive and his rejection of natural law per se. In seeking to discover law in the context of settling rights in particular cases, looking to established rules and precedents while keeping in mind the basic maxims of justice, common law judges did not make natural law their only point of reference, but they also did not treat it as something they were free to ignore. This is not the only way a legal order can respect natural law, but it is a legitimate way, and one that has contributed to keeping natural law a living force in the English and American constitutional traditions.

Precedent

A **precedent** is a principle or rule established in a previous legal case that is either binding on or persuasive for a court or other tribunal when deciding subsequent cases with similar issues or facts. Common-law legal systems place great value on deciding cases according to consistent principled rules, so that similar facts will yield similar and predictable outcomes, and observance of precedent is the mechanism by which that goal is attained. The principle by which judges are bound to precedents is known as **stare decisis** (a Latin phrase with the literal meaning of "*Let the decision stand*"). Common-law precedent is a third kind of law, on equal footing with statutory law (that is, statutes and codes enacted by legislative bodies) and subordinate legislation (that is, regulations promulgated by executive branch agencies, in the form of delegated legislation (in UK parlance) or regulatory law (in US parlance)).

Case law, in common-law jurisdictions, is the set of decisions of adjudicatory tribunals or other rulings that can be cited as precedent. In most countries, including most European countries, the term is applied to any set of rulings on law, which is guided by previous rulings, for example, previous decisions of a government agency. Essential to the development of case law is the publication and indexing of decisions for use by lawyers, courts, and the general public, in the form of law reports. While all decisions are precedent (though at varying levels of authority as discussed throughout this article), some become "leading cases" or "landmark decisions" that are cited especially often.

Generally speaking, a legal precedent is said to be:

- **applied** (if precedent is binding) / **adopted** (if precedent is persuasive), if the principles underpinning the previous decision are accordingly used to evaluate the issues of the subsequent case;
- **distinguished**, if the principles underpinning the previous decision is found specific to, or premised upon, certain factual scenarios, and not applied to the subsequent case because of the absence or material difference in the latter's facts; or
- **overruled**, if the same or higher courts on appeal or determination of subsequent cases found the principles underpinning the previous decision erroneous in law or overtaken by new legislation or developments.

In contrast, civil law systems adhere to a legal positivism, where past decisions do not usually have the precedential, binding effect that they have in common law decision-making; the judicial review practiced by constitutional courts can be regarded as a notable exception.

Stare decisis

(/ˈstɛərri dɪˈsaɪsɪs, ˈstɑːreɪ/) is a legal principle by which judges are obligated to respect the precedent established by prior decisions. The words originate from the phrasing of the principle in the Latin maxim *Stare decisis et non quieta movere*: "to stand by decisions and not disturb the undisturbed". In a legal context, this means that courts should abide by precedent and not disturb settled matters. The principle can be divided into two components:

1. A decision made by a superior court, or by the same court in an earlier decision, is binding precedent that the court itself and all its inferior courts must follow.
2. A court may overturn its own precedent, but should do so only if a strong reason exists to do so, and even in that case, should be guided by principles from superior, lateral, and inferior courts.
3. The second principle, regarding persuasive precedent, reflects the broad precedent guidance a court may draw upon in reaching all of its decisions.

Case law in common-law systems

In the common-law tradition, courts decide the law applicable to a case by interpreting statutes and applying precedent, which record how and why prior cases have been decided. Unlike most civil-law systems, common-law systems follow the doctrine of *stare decisis*, by which most courts are bound by their own previous decisions in similar cases, and all lower courts should make decisions consistent with previous decisions of higher courts.[6] For example, in England, the High Court and the Court of Appeal are each bound by their own previous decisions, but the Supreme Court of the United Kingdom is able to deviate from its earlier decisions, although in practice it rarely does so.

Generally speaking, higher courts do not have direct oversight over day-to-day proceedings in lower courts, in that they cannot reach out on their own initiative (*sua sponte*) at any time to reverse or overrule decisions of the lower courts. Normally, the burden rests with litigants to appeal rulings (including those in clear violation of established case law) to the higher courts. If a judge acts against precedent and the case is not appealed, the decision will stand.

A lower court may not rule against a binding precedent, even if the lower court feels that the precedent is unjust; the lower court may only express the hope that a higher court or the legislature will reform the rule in question. If the court believes that developments or trends in legal reasoning render the precedent unhelpful, and wishes to evade it and help the law evolve, the court may either hold that the precedent is inconsistent with subsequent authority, or that the precedent should be "distinguished: by some material difference between the facts of the cases. If that decision goes to appeal, the appellate court will have the opportunity to review both the precedent and the case under appeal, perhaps overruling the previous case law by setting a new precedent of higher authority. This may happen several times as the case works its way through successive appeals. Lord Denning, first of the High Court of Justice, later of the Court of Appeal, provided a famous example of this evolutionary process in his development of the concept of estoppel starting in the *High Trees* case: *Central London Property Trust Ltd v. High Trees House Ltd* [1947] K.B. 130.

Judges may refer to various types of persuasive authority to reach a decision in a case. Widely cited nonbinding sources include legal encyclopedias such as *Corpus Juris Secundum* and *Halsbury's Laws of England*, or the published work of the Law Commission or the American Law Institute. Some bodies are given statutory powers to issue guidance with persuasive authority or similar statutory effect, such as the Highway Code.

In federal or multijurisdictional law systems, conflicts may exist between the various lower appellate courts. Sometimes these differences may not be resolved and distinguishing how the law is applied in one district, province, division or appellate department may be necessary. Usually, only an appeal accepted by the court of last resort will resolve such differences, and for many reasons, such appeals are often not granted.

Any court may seek to distinguish its present case from that of a binding precedent, to reach a different conclusion. The validity of such a distinction may or may not be accepted on appeal. An appellate court may also propound an entirely new and different analysis from that of junior courts, and may or may not be bound by its own previous decisions, or in any case may distinguish the decisions based on significant differences in the facts applicable to each case. Or, a court may view the matter before it as one of "first impression", not governed by any controlling precedent.[7]

When various members of a multi-judge court write separate opinions, the reasoning may differ; only the *ratio decidendi* of the majority becomes binding precedent. For example, if a 12-member court splits 5-2-3-2 in four different opinions on several different issues, whatever reasoning commands seven votes on each specific issue, and the seven-judge majorities may differ issue-to-issue. All may be cited as persuasive (though of course opinions that concur in the majority result are more persuasive than dissents).

Quite apart from the rules of precedent, the weight actually given to any reported opinion may depend on the reputation of both the court and the judges with respect to the specific issue. For example, in the United States, the Second Circuit (New York and surrounding states) is especially respected in commercial and securities law, the Seventh Circuit (in Chicago), especially Judge Posner, is highly regarded on antitrust, and the District of Columbia Circuit is highly regarded on administrative law,

The African Diaspora

The African diaspora refers to the many communities of people of African descent dispersed throughout the world as a result of historic movements. The majority of African dispersal resulted from the Arab and Atlantic slave trades – the largest forced migrations in history. An estimated 11 million Africans were dispersed from the Atlantic slave trade from Western Africa (e.g., Ghana, Nigeria) and Central Africa (e.g., Congo, Cameroon) and an estimated 10 to 80 million from the **Arabic slave trade.** Despite popular association with the United States, only 5% of African slaves went to America while the remaining 95% went to Central America, South America and the Caribbean . Like African- Americans, other Africans in the Diaspora (e.g., Afro-Cubans, Afro-Brazilians, Afro-Costa Ricans, etc.) face challenges in their countries, and share a common history.

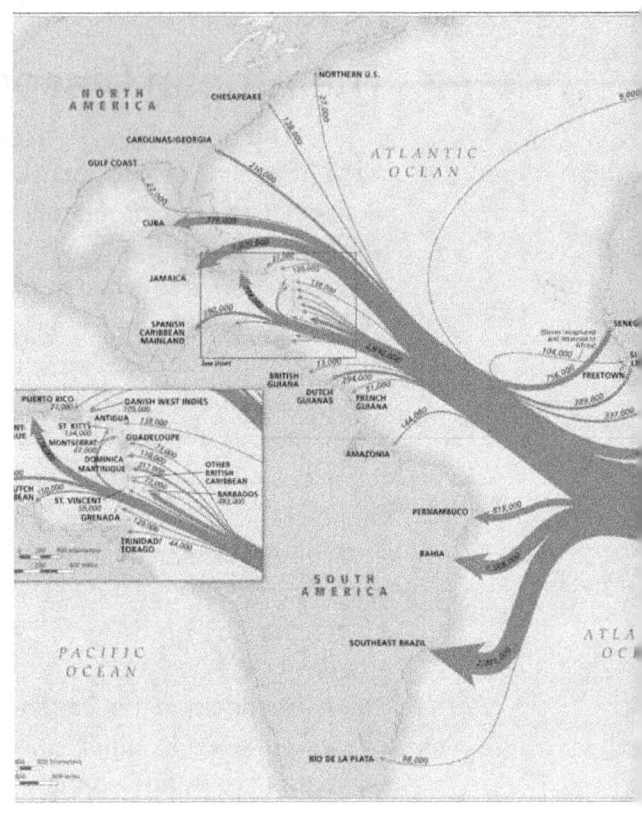

Map of Atlantic Slave Trade Movements

The African diaspora has a population of 140 million while Africa has a population of 1.2 billion. The most populated countries in the African diaspora include Brazil, Colombia, America, Dominican Republic, and Haiti. There is a connection among the descendants of slaves in the African Diaspora as their ancestors came from similar areas in Africa and survived a similar fate; slavery and colonization. Essentially they were taken to different countries around the world, disconnected from one another and their homelands.

African history does not begin with slavery, Africa's contributions to the development of mathematics, astronomy, medicine, architecture, philosophy, civilization, etc. are largely ignored. For instance, many notable Greek philosophers spent years in Africa learning from African philosophers who practiced philosophy long before the rise of Greek philosophy. Africa is home to many diverse countries and cultures, all with their own unique history. Many of the kingdoms of Africa are unknown; let us take a look at some.

The Axum Empire was a dominant power in what is now Ethiopia and Eritrea. From 100 to 940AD, the Axum Empire was one of four global superpowers along with Rome, China, and Persia and extended its influence as far as India and China.

The Benin Kingdom existed in what is now southern Nigeria, and achieved significant accomplishments in technology, architecture, science, art, administration, town-planning, astronomy, and more.

The Kingdom of Kush was an African kingdom where kings ruled as Pharaohs. This is known as the 25th dynasty of Egypt which was an influential time of renaissance in Egypt.

The silencing of Africa's history and achievement was established to support its occupation, division, and colonization from European powers known as the scramble for Africa– a race for Africa's resources and land.

THE MAD SCRAMBLE FOR AFRICA

-Scramble For Africa

As powerfully explained by Mallence Bart Williams here the West depends on Africa and this exploitation is still visible today in international powers disguised as charitable while actually concerned with the exploitation of resources. In terms of resources Africa is the richest continent

For those in the African diaspora, coming to terms with their heritage and not knowing where in Africa they come from can be a painful experience. For example, an Afro-Cuban thinking about her history: "What tribe do I belong to?", "Am I Nigerian?", "Am I Sierra Leonean?",
"Where is my family in Africa?", "What is my African culture?". This, she may never know as there were no records taken of slaves. She is disconnected from her true African culture. She may never beat the drum of her ancestors, wear the regalia of her foremothers, feel the traditional land of her people, or dance to her traditional music. This realization can cause great pain. At the same time, she is forced to accept a new culture: a culture that once saw her as a commodity, a culture that caused her so much pain, a culture that may or may not reject her. Africans in the diaspora and indigenous Africans, who were once joint in space and time are geographically disconnected.

Though, many cultures in the African Diaspora are traced with African influence – the Dominicans merengue, African Jamaican cuisine, African American music, and so forth. Cultures in the African *diaspora strive to re-capture what was lost from their global scattering and colonization. Many who are accustomed to being regarded as simply black are adventuring for terminology that categorizes them as individuals who are members of a larger culture which does not simply reflect the colour of their skin. For Africans in the Diaspora, decolonization involves reclaiming their African identity that was stolen from them and dispelling the negative views of Africa they have been socialized to hold under colonization, seeing Africa for its true beauty.*

This reality was but a component of the birthing of Pan-Africanism – an intellectual movement fathered by many distinguished persons, including Jamaica's Marcus Garvey

Pan-Africanism is a political doctrine, as well as a movement, with the aim of unifying and uplifting African nations and the African Diaspora as a universal African community. Pan-Africanism aims to build solidarity and unity among all people of African

Descent to promote social, political and economic success. In essence, Pan-Africanism holds that Africans and Africans in the Diaspora share not only a history, but common destiny.

Ending on the words of Teresa H. Clark from her speech on Bridging the Diaspora Divide – Honour the success of those within the diaspora. I think about when Alek Wek graced the first cover of Vogue Magazine, we were all South Sudanese, I think about when Kofi Annan became Secretary General of the United Nations we were all Ghanaian, when Barack Obama was elected president of the United States, the texts and emails I got from across the continent, we were all African American and today forty eight hours after we lost one of the worlds greatest leaders we are all South African, as we think about Madiba (Nelson Mandela) he is often counted in one of two ways clearly he belongs to his people of south Africa but he is so much bigger than that, he is one for the ages who belongs to the world but I am going to ask this group here today to join me claiming him as apart of Africa and the Diaspora- he is ours.

"LETS GET AWAY FROM THE WHY AND FOCUS ALL ENERGY ON THE HOW"

UNITY VOW

Defenders of Truth, Sovereignty and liberation. Guardian Families, serving the one. From across all the Multiverses I call upon my Guardian families to join me now. My unification is demonstrated in the waves of Omni Love. I round my heart tone to you now. My energy template is renewed and forever perpetuated in the Eternally Sustained Light. My Alchemical container is consecrated and dedicated to the purpose of One and I endeavor to be the Knower of GOD Source and then be the Way shower of the Divine. Please sustain me in the Eternal power of my Consecration.

I have asked for your Gatekeeping in order to hold my mission, my highest purpose in service to the One Light, my Source, the living light code. My intention is Unification-the cosmic Christ Principle-as in Energetic Reality, here and no.

I request the handshake to fortify my spiritual links through the Universal Cosmic Trinity, and into the core of one, the zero point GOD matrix, that which is the source of my Genesis. With deep reverence for all of life, Dear Divine Breath you living life codes into my created form. I set my intention now to be remembered to that which I AM, fully, completely GOD, Sovereign, Free!

I state my mutual purpose as One, please resurrect all inorganic and artificial patterns to the Organic Living Light now, and to that I say, Thank You Divine I AM the Living Eternal Light, and so it is lovingly deared.

HISTORY

King James the 1st of England was originally King James 6th of Scotland. He was the son of a black father and a colored mother both of royal blood. Without the necessary background, this may sound like a far-fetched story motivated by a crazy story to identify black heroes in Spain and southern Europe in 711CE, significant numbers of black people found their way into northern European countries such as Scotland, Ireland, France and Denmark. The nations of Scotland and Ireland were, since the beginning of the first millennium, had significant numbers of blacks in Scotland wielding political power as the kings and rulers. It is also from the preponderance of black people in Ireland in the medieval period that the term "black Irish" has continued to be used to this day. After the downfall of the moors in Granada, Spain, the white countries of Europe took a special interest in Scotland because there was a thriving black population there. Unlike the moors in Southern Europe who were moslems, the Scottish blacks were christians and therefore could not victimized on grounds of religion. They also wielded significant military power. To neutralize black influence in Scotland the neighboring white nations adopted the strategy of white washing the line of the black kings of Scotland. They entered into treaties with the Scottish kings that would ensure intermarriages between white princesses of the northern countries and the black kings of Scotland and their heirs. These were arranged marriages that would be overlooked by the Catholic church King James the 4th of Scotland was made to marry Margaret, the daughter of King Henry the 7th of England. England was then still under the Roman Catholic church and it was King Henry the 8th of England who would later break away from the Catholic church to form the Anglican church. It was from James the 4th arranged marriage with Margaret that the Scottish kings began having a legitimate shot at kingship in England. James the 5th was born to Margaret and would also be made to marry two white French women and his second wife was Mary the daughter of the Duke of Guise. This marriage gave birth to a daughter she would name Mary and would inherit the Scottish kingdom after the death of her father James the 5th. She was known as Mary the queen of Scotland. Mary was a Catholic and the queen of England hated her for this and also the fact that Mary had a legitimate claim to the English throne through her ancestors Henry 7th and grandmother Margaret. It was arranged that Mary (queen of Scots) be married to Edward the son of the British king, Henry 8th. In response, Mary's mother, the daughter of the Duke of Guise, a Catholi, condemned the arrangement and the Queen of the Scots had to decline the marriage. From then on, Italy, France, and England began battling for influence for the Scottish kingdom, Mary's mother as a daughter of a French Duke had been very influential during Queen Mary's reign, but when she eventually died, the Queen of Scotland became isolated and vulnerable. In 1565, Queen Mary was married by her cousin, a black Scottish man of the royal family who was called Darnley. Darnley was killed in 1567 by the white rivals of the Queen, but he had left Queen Mary a male heir of her own lineage, Queen Mary's son was born a few months before his father's murder and he was named James the 6th. James the 6th was, therefore, the son of a black man and a coloured woman. The black man's gene is dominant to the white man's gene because the latter is recessive. When the two races meet in miscegenation, it is the white side which is forced to die (recess); however the offspring loses some black characteristics such as kinkiness of hair and darkness of skin but only to a small extent. This means James the 6th being a son of a black man and a coloured woman, probably looked no different from any black man we see today. The white nations were angered firstly by Mary,s refusal to marry Edward of England and for that they murdered a man named Beaton who was an advisor to Mary and her mother. When Mary provided a black heir, she undid the generations of genetic whitewashing that the whites had forced the Scottish kings to succumb to. Darnley was killed for fathering Mary's black heir Mary to face imprisonment and Queen Elizabeth laid a heavy hand on her because she was Catholic and she was a potential competitor to the throne of England. In 1587, Mary the Queen of Scotland was executed by order of Queen Elizabeth of England. King James the 6th began ruling Scotland. Although angered by his mother's death he did not retaliate against England; rather he looked at the situation diplomatically and realized that the Catholic church had no place in the region of northern Europe anymore. All the other nations of northern europe to with the exception of France were not affiliated to protestant churches. The Caucasian whites who were once known as barbarians had a bad history with the Catholic church and had been exploited and treated less than humans by the Roman popes and priests for over 1000 years. For this reason, protestant churches were popular in northern Europe and they were named " protestant" because they were in protest to the Roman Catholic church which was considered orthodox. King James the 6th thus made ties with the Anglican church through associating closely with the English. Very quickly he became an ally of England and an enemy of the Catholic church. Once England and Scotland were cooperating with each other France could not do much against the Scotts on behalf of the Catholics. This angered authorities of the Roman Catholic church because the church had lost its dominion over the northern territories of Europe. Meanwhile King James was becoming great in his own governance and having a general sense of kingship which was lacking in many European nations at the time. He treasured nobility, but conducted his duties with dignity and humility. His government was orderly and popular. The kingdom of England was at this time lacking male heirs yet there was a descendant of King Henry the 7th (through Margaret) thriving in Scotland. Before long, it became obvious that England was going to be under king James. In 1603 king James the 6th of Scotland was crowned king James the 1st of England Scotland, England and Ireland were now under his rule.   -simba jama-

So now that we know King James the 1st of England 6th of Scotland Ireland was a black man let's get into some of the things he did during his reign as king of three countries. Getting straight to it one of the most famous developments was the new Authorized English translation of the bible published in 1611 which became known as the AKJV which stands for the Authorized King James version with the Apocrypha. The bible is the most important book in the history of WESTERN CIVILIZATION,and the most difficult to interpret. It has been the vehicle of continual conflict with every interpretation reflecting passionately held views that have affected not merely religion but politics,art and even science. This unique edition offers an exciting new approach to the most influential of all English biblical texts, the Authorized King James Version complete with the Apocrypha.

Now I know that word Apocrypha is new to you,or it might be old to you let's go into some definitions-it comes from the Greek word meaning "hidden or secret" Originally, the term was reserved for books with content considered too sacred and grand to make accessible to the general public-The history of the term's usage indicates that it referred to a body of esoteric writings that were at first prized,later tolerated,and finally excluded. Esoteric-the quality of having an inner or secret meaning. The term and it's correlative exoteric were first applied in the Ancient Greek mysteries to those who were initiated eso-within and to those who were not(exo-outside) repeatedly-something only understood by a chosen group.

14 Books of the Apocrypha

1 Esdras (Vulgate 3 Esdras)
2 Esdras (Vulgate 4 Esdras)
Tobit
Judith ("Judith" in Geneva
Rest of Esther (Vulgate Esther 10:4-16:24)
Wisdom
Ecclesiasticus(also known as Sirach)
Baruch and the Epistle of Jeremy("Jeremiah" in Geneva)
Call part of Vulgate Baruch
The songs of the three holy children
The history of Susana
Bel and the dragon
The prayer for Manassas
1 Maccabees
2 Maccabees

Now there are more books that were taken out due to other religions' decisions to conquer other nations and build their nation up! For instance the Jews and protestants Roman Catholics.
Some cultures use these books for their own take over by hiding the knowledge from the original design people and changing the language and culture to make their own.

Let's go back to time and talk about Roman emperor Constantine who is known as Constantine he ruled from 306 to 337 AD Born in Naissus, Dacia Mediterranean he was a the son of flavius Constantine (a Roman army officer born in Dacia ripensis who had been one of the four emperors of the tetrarchy). His mother Helena was Greek and of low birth. Constantine served with distinction under the Romans emperor's Diocletian and Galerius. He began by campaigning in the esteem provinces (against barbarians and the Persians) before he was recalled in the west (in AD 305) to fight alongside his father in Britain. After his father's death in 306 Constantine became emperor he was acclaimed by his army at Eboracum (York, England). He emerged victorious in the civil wars against emperor Maxentius and Licinius to become the sole ruler of the Roman Empire by 324 Constantine was the first Roman emperor to convert to Christianity. Although he lived much of his life as a pagan and later as a catechumen he began to favor christianity in 312 finally became a Christian and being baptized by either Eusebius of nicomedia, an Arian bishop as attested by many notable Arian historical figures or Pope Sylvester 1 which is maintained by the Catholic Church and the Coptic Orthodox church. He played an influential role in the proclamation of the Edict of Milan in 313 which declared tolerance for Christianity in the Roman empire; he convoked the first council of Nicaea in 325 which produced the statement of Christian belief known as the Nicene Creed. The church of the holy sepulchre was built on his orders at the purported site of Jesus (aka Isa) or (Yeshua) in Jerusalem and was deemed the holiest place in all Christianson. The papal claim to temporal power in the high middle ages was based on the fabricated donation of constantine. He has historically been referred to as the "First Christian Emperor" and he did favor the Christian church. While some modern scholars debate his beliefs and even his compensation of Christianity he is venerated as a saint in Eastern in Christianity and did much for pushing Christianity towards the mainstream of Roman culture. The age of Constantine marked a distinct epoch in the history of the Roman empire and a pivotal moment in the transition from classical antiquity to the middle ages He built a new imperial residence at the city of Byzantine and Constantinople after himself. It subsequently became the capital of the empire for more than a thousand years. The later Eastern Roman Empire was referred to as the Byzantine Empire by modern historians. It's more immediate political legacy was that he replaced Diocletian's Tetrarchy with the De facto principle of dynastic succession by leaving the empire to his son's and other members of the Constantinian dynasty.

Let's define De facto-("in fact") describes practices that exist in reality, even though they are not officially recognized by laws. It is commonly used to refer to what happens in practice, in contrast with de jure ("by laws") which refers to things that happen according to law.

In "Jurisprudence" which means-legal theory is the theoretical study of the propriety of law. Modern Jurisprudence began in the 18th century. Three distinct branches of thought in general Jurisprudence Ancient Natural law-which elaborates on the idea that there are rational objective limits to the power of legislative rulers The foundation of law are accessible through reason and it is from these laws of nature that human laws gain whatever force they have.

Analytic Jurisprudence(clarificatory Jurisprudence) rejects natural law's fusing of what law is and what it ought to be. It espouses the use of a neutral point of view and descriptive language when referring to aspects of legal systems it encompasses such theories of Jurisprudence as legal positivism which holds that there is no necessary connection between law and morality and that the force of law comes from basic social facts and legal realism which argues that the real world practice of law determines what law is the law having the force that it does because of what legislators, lawyers and judges do with it.

I've talked about the emperor Constantine at the time, I'm gonna leave him for now and jump into the Pope at that time of Constantine full rule of all the Tetrarchy which was Pope Sylvester 1. Later on in the book will be the breakdown of Natural law which is basically universal law and analytical law that have to do with the De facto principle.

So the Donation of Constantine is a document fabricated in the second half of the eight century purporting to be a record left by the emperor himself of his conversion, the profession of his new faith and the privileges he conferred on Pope Sylvester 1 himself, his clergy and his successors. According to it Pope Sylvester was offered the imperial crown which however, he refused, a story in Giuseppe Pitrè S collection of Sicilian fables recounts the legend as follows: Constantine the king wants to take a second wife, and ask Sylvester, Sylvester denies him permission calling on heaven as a witness; Constantine threatens him and Sylvester rather than gives in escapes into the woods not long after Constantine falls I'll when he is desperate of ever regaining his health he has a dream which commands him to send for Sylvester he obeys and Sylvester receives Constantine's messengers in his cage and swiftly baptizes them, whereafter (showing them several miracles) he is led back to Constantine whom he baptizes also and cures. In this story Constantine and his entourage are not pagans but Jews. Another legend has Sylvester slaying a dragon. He is often depicted with the dying beasts.

The United States is a Corporation PERIOD!! Let's look at modern day Corporations for example Amazon, Walmart, just to name a few each one of these corporations have a President, Vice president Treasurer also a board of directors subcommittees etc..... Now let's look at the US. which means the United States. There is a President, Vice President Treasurer, all subcommittees like every government organization like social security administration social services these federal buildings or organizations like the CIA police department FBI are sub committees of the US. or in other words a part of the US. system or Corporation. This money system has been flipped in a way where we are always the borrower and not the lender. So the US corporations want you to always depend on their system ITS FRAUD!! Let's define what fraud is-wrongful or criminal deception intended to result in a financial or personal gain-another definition is deceit,trickery, specifically intentional perversion of truth in order to induce another to part with something of value or to surrender a legal right to b. An act of deceiving or misrepresentation TRICK!!

The Rothschild have been in control of the world's money supply for more than two centuries, Donald V. Watkins writes, yet most Americans have never heard of them. The Rothschild's family was the dominant power in European investment banking and brokerages in the nineteenth century. Family members held seats in parliament and in the house of Lords they became Barons in London and they founded the Rothschild national history museum. The Rothschild's are a family of Jewish financiers. By 1815, Nathan Mayer Rothschild controlled the bank of England and declared "I care not what puppet is placed upon the throne of England to rule the empire on which the sun never sets. The man who controls Britain's Empire and I control the

British money supply "This became the Rothschild family mantra--control the world by controlling the world's money supply.
By the end of the nineteenth century. The Rothschild family controlled half of the world's wealth. In 1791, the Rothschild's family gained control of America's money supply through Alexander Hamilton(the family's agent in George Washington's cabinet) when the family established a central bank in the U.S. named the first bank of the United States which received a 20 year charter from congress in 1791.
When Congress refused to renew the charter in 1812 the Rothschild threatened the U.S. with a most disastrous war in Britain. The U.S. stood firm following through on their threat. A second war broke out between the U.S. and Britain. The British war effort was financed by the Rothschilds. When the war ended 1815 the U.S. finances were in shambles.
By 1816, Congress passed a bill authorizing a second Rothschild's-dominated central bank with a 20 year charter. Named the Second Bank of America, this bank gave the Rothschild's control of the money supply again.
In 1823, the Rothschild's took control over the financial operations of the Catholic church worldwide.
In 1832, President Andrew Jackson led a successful effort by congress to retake control of America's money supply from the Rothschild's by

refusing to renew the charter for the second bank of America. Not until 1913 would the Rothschild's be able to set up their third central bank of America. In the meantime, beginning in 1875, the Rothschild's acted through their New York banking partner. Jacob Schiff, at the banking house of Kuhn Loeb, and Co, financed John D Rockefeller's standard oil company, Edward R. Harrimans railroad empire and Andrew Carnegie's steel empire using Rothschild's money.
The Rothschild's also helped New York financier J.P. Morgan and the Drexel's and Biddles of Philadelphia establish European branches of their respective banks in exchange for allowing Rothschild's to control the banking industry in New York and therefore America.
In 1913 the Rothschild's established their last and current central bank in America-The Federal Reserve bank. This independent bank regulates and controls America's money supply and monetary policies. Even though the federal reserve is overseen by a board of governors appointed by the president of the United States, the bank's real control still resides with the Rothschilds family.
Jekyll Island was the location of a meeting in November 1910 in which draft legislation was written to create a central banking system for the United States. Following the panic of 1907 banking reform became a major issue in the United States. "Picture a party of the nation's greatest bankers stealing out of New York on a private railroad car

under cover of darkness, stealthily riding hundreds of miles South embarking on a mysteriously launch, sneaking onto an island deserted by all but a few servants, living there a full week under such rigid secrecy that the names of not one of them was once mentioned, lest the servants learn the identity and disclose to the world for the first time the real story of how the famous Aldrich currency reports the foundation of our new currency system was, written...The utmost secrecy was enjoined upon all. The public must not glean a hint of what was to be done.

Senator Aldrich notified each one to go quietly into a private care of which the railroad has received orders to draw up on an island unfrequented platform, off the party set. New York's ubiquitous reporters had been foiled Nelson (Aldrich) had confirmed to Henry Frank, Paul and Piatt that he was to keep them locked up at jekyll island out of the rest of the world, until they evolved and compiled a scientific currency system for the United States, the real birth of the present Federal Reserve System the plan done on Jekyll island in the conference with the Paul, Frank and Henry... Warburg is the link that binds that Aldrich system and the present together. He more than any other man has made the system possible as a working reality!

From the beginning, the government was indebted to European bankers as a result of the revolution.

1933 was also when the United States went bankrupt for the third time's previous year was 1789(this was the year the constitution was formed so the states could sign on as security for the Feds debt)-1861 the Southern states did not want to sign on to another pledging of assets to pay the federal government debt.

Also in 1933 with the HJR that took all the gold, all the true money, all the property(and instituted eminent domain and property/taxes dividend land titles and instituted the income tax to control the labor of the people. In addition HJR is when they instituted birth certificates to control the people and have the future American people become collateral for all the federal government debt.

Your BC is the title to your body and was and is still being pledged as an asset. The holder has the right to the taxes and fines,fees that you pay to the government through judgment, court cases, payroll income taxes property taxes etc.

Your name is the most important powerful word on this planet next to your signature which is the second most important written words on this planet. Everything going forward please believe, either is born or taken away from our name. It's a powerful weapon. I want you to understand it or this. Your name is important PERIOD!!

Let's get into HJR-192 for a minute..HJR stands for house joint resolution which passes by when the Senate and the house of representatives pass a law together house joint resolution. Let's look a a specific law that congress passed which is HJR-192 Public Law 73-10 Laws that govern electronic transfer instruments and money

The Federal Government took all lawful money out of circulation in 1933 but congress had to provide the people with a remedy. Public law chap 48 48 statute 112 discharges all debts, public and private dollar for dollar. This has been one of the best kept secrets in the bankruptcy nation.

They took everything including all property and titles to property and left us only with an ability to discharge debt and create money through our signature and they ever bothered to tell us.

We create money when we apply for bank loans with our signature. It is our signature and credit in our ability to work that creates the money of the account and this has been the case since 1933. The bank's have a monopoly to our credit and for this "service" they charge principal and interest on nonexistent money all the time giving the impression they lent us their money and this is fraud because they never revealed where the money came from. This is true for credit accounts and mortgages. A Lot of people don't know that there is no real money to pay debt. Federal reserves notes are the United States form of currency but it is not money, it is debt notes and legally you cannot pay a debt with debt notes. Each and every person who is a U.S. citizen has the remedy for payment of debt. It has just been kept from the public eye. Each person has

unlimited credit due to them for the removal of the gold and silver standard. Research this and you will find out.
All debts have already been paid, each institution that demands your involuntary servitude federal reserve notes holds you in bondage. You are willingly but unknowingly a slave.
To deny the procedure to discharge public debt is fraud,conspiracy,racketeering,collusion,theft of public funds Dishonor in commerce.
To estoppel anyone from gaining such knowledge is Fraud,conspiracy,racketeering,collusion,theft of public funds,and a Dishonor in commerce.
A taxpayer has an interest in the general funds held by the U.S. Treasury. Most Americans are authorized representatives of their legal entity known as the TAXPAYER AND EACH has an interest in said funds. This was decided by the Supreme Court.
Everyone who hold a CREDIT CARD on behalf of the TAXPAYER(your name in all caps) demand the guidance of ANY said officer of any CREDIT CARD company the name institutionor other on how to correctly utilize discharge ,use,full disclosure of said procedure to credit the legal entities account with the discharge or offset of public debt. CREDIT that is due to the taxpayer upon a signature of said name in the unlimited commercial capacity.
As authorized representatives of their legal entity they are entitled to write and tender lawful notes common practice for many years.

This resolution declared that any obligation requiring "payment" in gold or a particular kind of coin or currency or in an amount in money policy and...Every obligation heretofore or hereafter incurred, shall be discharged upon payment dollar for dollar, in any coin or currency which at the time of payment is legal tender for public and private debts.

A farm control bill around the same time period had attached to it a clause making Federal Reserve notes legal tender. In 1937 the supreme court struck down the farm control Act, thus carrying with it the legal tender status the federal reserve notes. Prior to 1933 Federal reserve notes were used for intra-bank transfer. Around 1945 Congress passed a bill which called for the withdrawal of Federal reserve notes from public circulation; but they are still with us *NOTE- that the words do not talk about "payment" of debt but clearly states that every obligation.....shall be discharged; The court explained the legal distinction between the words "payment" and "discharge" There is a distinction between a "debt discharge" and "debt paid" When discharged the debt still exist though divested of its character as a legal obligation during the operation of the discharge.

Something of the original vitality of the debt continues to exist, which may be transferred even though the transferee takes it subject to its disability incident to the discharge. The fact that it carries something which may be a consideration for a new promise to pay, so as to make an otherwise worthless promise a legal obligation, makes it the subject of transfer by assignment. It is clear that, as a result of HJR-192 and from that day forward (June 5 1933) no one has been able to pay a debt. The only thing they can also is tender in transfer of debt and the debt is perpetual. The suspension of the gold standard, and prohibition against paying debts, removed the substance for our common law to operate on, and created a void as far as the law is concerned. This substance was replaced with a Public National Credit System where debt is money(The Federal reserve calls it "monetized debt") over which the only Admiralty and Maritime. HJR-192 was implemented immediately. The day after President Roosevelt signed the resolution the Treasury offered the public new government securities, minus the traditional payable in gold and silver coin and a tender in payment of debt-but this Article does not contain an absolute prohibition against the states making something else a tender in transfer of debt.

HJR-192 prohibits payment of debt and substitutes in its place, a discharge of an obligation--thereby not only subverting, but totally bypassing the "absolute prohibition" so carefully engineered into the constitution. There is now nothing for this Article to operate on, just as there is nothing for common law to operate on Perpetual debt, bills,notes,cheques,and credits fall within a totally different jurisdiction than contemplated by Article 1, section 10 clause 1--and that jurisdiction belongs exclusively to the law of Admiralty and Maritime. HJR-192 places every person who deals in the public national credit in the legal position of a merchant,and the only jurisdiction for any controversy involving this subject matter is Admiralty and Maritime.

If all the assets of the United States have been hypothecated to the Federal Reserve "pool" as security for the Maritime loan and insurance underwriting policy

Question #1 If the United States "dies" (or is merged) under a One world government, who get the "pool"

Question #2 If the Federal Reserve "dies" by way of getting it's character rescinded, who gets the "pool"

--Answer-- Should a Federal Reserve bank be dissolved or go into liquidation,any surplus remaining after the payment of all debts, dividend requirements as hereinbefore provided, and the par value of the stock, shall be paid to and become the property of the United States and shall be singularly applied! Thank you educationcenter2000.

HJR-192 automatically extended the privilege to renege on debts to every person using the Federal Reserve banking system. I know your asking what renege mean let's define it Renege means- go back on a promise, undertaking,or contract

Synonyms- default on,fail to honor, go back on,break,break out of,pull out of,withdraw from, retreat from,Welsh on,backtrack on,repudiate,retract,go back on one's word, breaks one's word, break's one's promise, do an about face, cop out, rat on.

Charter of Maryland 1632 Charles I King of England,Scotland,Ireland as it reads:

& Familys unto the said Province, with convenient shipping and fitting Provisions, and there to settle themselves, dwell and inhabit, and to build, and fortify Castles, Forts, and other Places of Strength, for the publick; and their own private Defence, at the Appointment of the said now Lord *Baltemore*, & his Heirs, the Statute ~~of~~ concerning Fugitives, or any other whatsoever to the contrary of the Premises, in any wise notwithstanding.

And we will also, and of our more special Grace, for us, our Heirs and Successors, we do straightly enjoin, constitute, ordain, and command that the said Province shall be of our Allegiance, and that all and singular the Subjects and Liegepeople of us, our Heirs and Successors, transported, or to be transported into the said Province, and the Children of them, and of such as shall descend from them, there already born, or hereafter to be born, be, and shall be Denizens and Lieges of us, our Heirs, and Successors, of our Kingdom of *England*, and *Ireland*, and be in all Things held, treated,

People born in Maryland *made Denizens of England.*

our Kingdom of *England*, and other our Dominions, may inherit, or otherwise purchase, receive, take, have, hold, buy, & possess, & them may occupy, & enjoy, give, sell, aliene, and bequeath, as likewise, all Liberties, Franchises, and Priviledges, of this our Kingdom of *England*, freely, quietly, and peaceably, have & possess, occupy and enjoy, as our liege people, born, or to be born, within our said Kingdom of *England*, without the let, Molestation, vexation, trouble or Grievance, of us, our Heirs, and Successors: Any Statute, Act, Ordinance, or Provision to the contrary thereof not withstanding.

And furthermore, that our Subjects may be the rather encouraged to undertake this Expedition, with ready and chearfull Minds; know ye, that we of our special Grace, certain Knowledge, and meer Motion, do give & grant, by vertue of these presents, as well unto the said now Lord *Baltemore*, and his Heirs; as to all others that shall from Time to Time repair unto that Province, with a Purpose to inhabit there, or to trade with the

Licence to transport goods and merchandise.

Denization

Is an obsolete or defunct process in England and Ireland and the later Kingdom of Great Britain, the United Kingdom, and the British Empire, dating back to the 13th century, by which an alien (foreigner), through letters patent, became a **denizen**, thereby obtaining certain rights otherwise normally enjoyed only by the King's (or Queen's) subjects, including the right to hold land. The denizen was neither a subject (with citizenship or nationality) nor an alien, but had a status akin to permanent residency today. While one could become a subject via naturalisation, this required a private act of Parliament (or latterly of a colonial legislature); in contrast, denization was cheaper, quicker, and simpler. Denization fell into obsolescence when the British Nationality and Status of Aliens Act 1914 simplified the naturalisation process.

Denization occurred by a grant of letters patent, an exercise of the royal prerogative. Denizens paid a fee and took an oath of allegiance to the crown. For example, when Venetian mariner Gabriel Corbet was granted letters of denization in 1431 for service upon the seas to Henry V and Henry VI, he was required to pay 40 shillings into the hanaperfor the privilege.

The status of denizen allowed a foreigner to purchase property, although a denizen could not inherit property. Sir William Blackstone wrote "A denizen is a kind of middle state, between an alien and a natural-born subject, and partakes of both." The denizen had limited political rights: he could vote, but could not be a member of parliament or hold any civil or military office of trust. Denizenship has also been compared to the Roman *civitas sine suffragio*, although the rights of denizens were restricted by the Act of Settlement 1701, not by common or immemorial law.

Denization was expressly preserved by the Naturalisation Act 1870 and by s25 of the British Nationality and Status of Aliens Act 1914. According to the British Home Office, the last denization was granted to the Dutch painter Lawrence Alma-Tadema in 1873; the Home Office considered it obsolete when the Prince of Pless applied for it in 1933, and instructed him to apply for naturalisation instead. The British Nationality Act 1948, a major reform of citizenship law in Britain, made no mention of denization and neither abolished nor preserved the practice.

Denization, as an exercise of royal power, was applicable throughout the British dominion to all British subjects. That is, it was exercisable in the colonies. For example, denization occurred in the colony of New South Wales. As in Britain, the practice became obsolete to naturalisation, with the last known denization in 1848.

The term *denizen* may also refer to any national of a country, whether citizen or non-citizen, with a right to remain in and return to the country. In the United States, before they were made citizens by statute, unassimilated Native Americans, although born on U.S. soil, were not deemed to be citizens of the United States or any state, but of a domestic dependent nation contained within the United States but whose members are not even nationals of it, but denizens of it, with a right to remain in and return to their reserved territories.

Inhabitants-- A person or animal that lives in or occupies a place

    A person who fulfills the requirements for legal residency

Liege--Vassal bond to feudal service and allegiance

    A loyal subject

    A feudal superior to whom allegiance and service are due

The Declaration and Charter of rights August 14,-November 11, 1776

The Parliament of Great-Britain by declaratory act having assumed a right to make laws to bind the colonies in all sales whatsoever and is pursuant of such claim endeavoured by force of arms to subjugate the United Colonies to an unconditional submission to their will and power and having at length constrained them to craft themselves into independent states and to assume new forms of government.

We, therefore, the delegates of Maryland, in free and full Convention assembled taking into our most serious consideration the best means of establishing a good constitution in this state for the forer fondation and more permanent security thereof declare:

1. That all government of rights originates from the people is founded in compact only and

instituted solely for the good of the whole.
2. That persons entrusted with the legislature and executive powers are the trustees and servants of the public and as such accountable for their conduct wherefore whenever the ends of government are perverted and public liberty manifestly endangered by the legislative-singly or a treacherous combination of both those powers,the people may and of right ought to establish a new or reform the old government passive obedience is only due to laws of god and to laws of the land the doctrine of non-resistance against arbitrary powers and oppression is absurd slavish and destructive of the good and happiness of mankind
3. 16-That the inhabitants of Maryland are entitled to the common law of england and to the trial by jury according to the course of that law and to the benefit of such ofthe english statutes as existed at the time of their first emigration and which by experience have been found

applicable to their local and other circumstances and of such others as have been since introduced used and practiced by the courts of law or equity and to all acts of assembly in force prior to the first of June seventeen seventy four except such as have been or may be altered by acts of convention or this charter of rights and to all property derived from or under the charter granted by his majesty Charles the first of Cecilius Calvert baton of baltimore

4. 17-That every freeman for every injury dones to him in his goods lands or person by any other person ought to have remedy by the course of the law of the land and ought to have justice and right for the injury done to him freely without sale fully without any denial and speedily without delay according to the law of the land

5. 18-That the trial of facts where they arise is one of the greatest securities of the lives liberties and estate of the people

6. 38-That the city of Annapolis ought to have all its rights

privileges and benefits agreeable to its charter and the acts of assembly
7. 40-That monopolies in trade are odious contrary to the spirit of a free government and the principles of commerce and ought not to be suffered
8. 41-That no person hereafter imported into the state from Africa or any part of the British dominion ought to held in slavery under any pretense whatever and that no negro or mullatto slave ought to be brought into this state for sale from any part of the world
9. 43-That the resolve and proceedings of this and the several conditions held for this colony ought to continue and be in force as laws unless altered by this convention or by legislature of this state
10. 44-That the form of government to be established by this convention ought not to be altered change or abolished but in such manner as this Convention shall prescribe and direct

The Two U.S. Constitutions

Two Constitutions in the United States. 1st was suspended in favor of a Vatican Corporation in 1871

Since 1871 the United States president and the United States Congress has been playing politics under a different set of rules and policies. The American people do not know that there are two Constitutions in the United States. The first penned by the leaders of the newly independent states of the United States in 1776. On July 4, 1776, the people claimed their independence from Britain and Democracy was born. And for 95 years the United

States people were free and independent. That freedom ended in 1871 when the original "Constitution for the united states for America" was changed to the "THE CONSTITUTION OF THE UNITED STATES OF AMERICA".

The Congress realized that the country was in dire financial straits, so they made a financial deal with the devil – international bankers — (in those days, the Rothschilds of London) thereby incurring a DEBT to said bankers. The conniving international bankers were not about to lend the floundering nation any money without some serious stipulations. So, they devised a way of taking back control of the United States and thus, the Act of 1871 was passed. With no constitutional authority to do so, Congress created a separate form of government for the District of Columbia.

With the passage of "the Act of 1871" a city state (a state within a state) called the District of Columbia located on 10 sq miles of land in the heart of Washington was formed with its own flag and its own independent constitution – the United States' secret second constitution.

The flag of Washington's District of Columbia has 3 red stars, each symbolizing a city state within the three city empire. The three city empire consists of Washington D.C., London, and Vatican City. London is the corporate center of the three city states and controls the world economically. Washington's District of Columbia city state is in charge of the military, and the Vatican controls it all under the guise of spiritual guidance. Although geographically separate, the city states of London, the Vatican and the District of Columbia are one interlocking empire called "Empire of the City"

The constitution for the District of Columbia operates under tyrannical Vatican law known as "Lex Fori" (local law). When congress passed the act of 1871 it created a separate corporation known as THE UNITED STATES and corporate government for the District of Columbia. This treasonous act has unlawfully allowed the District of Columbia to operate as a corporation outside the original constitution of the United States and in total disregard of the best interests of the American citizens.

Obama-linked-to-Vatican

(POTUS Obama at the Vatican Corporate headquarters)

POTUS is the Chief Executive (president) of the Corporation of the United States operating as any other CEO of the corporation — governs w/a Board of Directors (cabinet officials) and managers (Senators/Congress) Obama as others before him is POTUS — operating as "vassal king" taking orders once again from "The City of London" through the RIIA (Royal Institute of Intl Affairs). The Illuminati (founded by The Society of Jesus or Jesuits, the largest Roman Catholic Religious Military Order headed by the Black Pope) created the Royal Institute of International Affairs (RIIA) in 1919. The American equivalent to the RIIA is the Council of Foreign Relations (CFR). The RIIA and CFR set up Round Table Groups (based on the King Arthur myths).

What did the Act of 1871 achieve? The ACT of 1871 put the United States back under British rule (which is under Vatican rule). The United States people lost their independence in 1871.

THE CONSTITUTION OF THE UNITED STATES OF AMERICA is the constitution of the incorporated UNITED STATES OF AMERICA. It operates in an economic capacity and has been used to fool the People into thinking it governs the Republic. It does not! Capitalization is NOT insignificant when one is referring to a legal document. This seemingly "minor" alteration has had a major impact on every subsequent generation of Americans. What Congress did by passing the Act of 1871 was create an entirely new document, a constitution for the government of the District of Columbia, an INCORPORATED government.

Instead of having absolute and unalienable rights guaranteed under the organic Constitution, we the people now have "relative" rights or privileges. One example is the Sovereign's right to travel, which has now been transformed (under corporate government policy) into a "privilege" that requires citizens to be licensed – driver's licenses and Passports. By passing the Act of 1871, Congress committed TREASON against the People who were Sovereign under the grants and decrees of the Declaration of Independence and the organic Constitution. The Act of 1871 became the FOUNDATION of all the treason committed by government officials.

As of 1871 the United States isn't a Country; It's a Corporation! In preparation for stealing America, the puppets of Britain's banking cabal had already created a second government, a Shadow Government designed to manage what "the people" believed was a democracy, but what really was an incorporated UNITED STATES. Together this chimera, this two-headed monster, disallowed "the people" all rights of sui juris. [you, in your sovereignty]

The U.S.A. is a Crown Colony. The U.S. has always been and remains a British Crown colony. King James I, is not just famous for translating the Bible into "The King James Version", but for signing the "First Charter of Virginia" in 1606 — which granted America's British forefathers license to settle and colonize America. The charter guaranteed future

Kings/Queens of England would have sovereign authority over all citizens and colonized land in America.

After America declared independence from Great Britain, the Treaty of Paris, signed on September 3, 1783 was signed. That treaty identifies the King of England as prince of U.S. "Prince George the Third, by the grace of God, king of Great Britain, France, and Ireland, defender of the faith, duke of Brunswick and Lunebourg, arch- treasurer and prince elector of the Holy Roman Empire etc., and of the United States of America"– completely contradicting premise that America won The War of Independence.

Article 5 of that treaty gave all British estates, rights and properties back to Britain.

It is agreed that Congress shall earnestly recommend it to the legislatures of the respective states to provide for the restitution of all estates, rights, and properties, which have been confiscated belonging to real British subjects; and also of the estates, rights, and properties of persons resident in districts in the possession on his Majesty's arms and who have not borne arms against the said United States. And that persons of any other description shall have free liberty to go to any part or parts of any of the thirteen United States and therein to remain twelve months unmolested in their endeavors to obtain the restitution of such of their estates, rights, and properties as may have been confiscated; and that Congress shall also earnestly recommend to the several states a reconsideration and revision of all acts or laws regarding the premises, so as to render the said laws or acts perfectly consistent not only with justice and equity but with that spirit of conciliation which on the return of the blessings of peace should universally prevail. And that Congress shall also earnestly recommend to the several states that the estates, rights, and properties, of such last mentioned persons shall be restored to them, they refunding to any persons who may be now in possession the bona fide price (where any has been given) which such persons may have paid on purchasing any of the said lands, rights, or properties since the confiscation.

And it is agreed that all persons who have any interest in confiscated lands, either by debts, marriage settlements, or otherwise, shall meet with no lawful impediment in the prosecution of their just rights.

It is becoming increasingly apparent to American citizens that government is no longer being conducted in accordance with the U.S. Constitution, or, within states, according to state constitutions. While people have recognized for more than 150 years that the rich and powerful often corrupt individual officials, or exert undue influence to get legislation passed that favors their interests, most Americans still cling to the naive belief that such corruption is exceptional, and that most of the institutions of society, the courts, the press, and law enforcement agencies, still largely comply with the Constitution and the law in important matters. They expect that these corrupting forces are disunited and in competition with one another, so that they tend to balance one another.

Mounting evidence makes it clear that the situation is far worse than most people think, that during the last several decades the U.S. Constitution has been effectively overthrown, and that it is now observed only as a façade to deceive and placate the masses. What has replaced it is what many call the Shadow Government – created with the illegal passing of the Act of 1871. It still, for the most part, operates in secret, because its control is not secure. The exposure of this regime and its operations must now become a primary duty of citizens who still believe in the Rule of Law and in the freedoms which this country is supposed to represent.

American Citizen or U.S. Citizen

There appears to be general misunderstanding by people in general as to the difference between a natural person and an artificial person. This document will explain that difference.

John Joseph Smith, is a natural, flesh and blood, person, created by God.

JOHN JOSEPH SMITH, is a U.S. corporate artificial person, U.S. citizen, created by the government.

In basic English grammar, a name spelled in upper and lower case, such as John Joseph Smith, is indicative of a flesh and blood man, a natural person.

> **Person.** *In general usage,* ***a human being (i.e. natural person)****, though by statute may include labor organizations, partnerships, associations,* ***corporations, legal representatives****, trustees, trustees in bankruptcy, or receivers.* Black's Law Dictionary 6th Ed.

On the other hand, a name spelled in all caps, such as JOHN JOSEPH SMITH, is indicative of an artificial person.

> **Artificial persons.** *Persons created and devised by human laws* for the purposes of society and government, *as distinguished from natural persons.* Corporations are examples of artificial persons. Black's 6th Ed.

> **U.S. v. Anthony 24 Fed. 829 (1873)**
> "The term resident and citizen of the United States is distinguished from a Citizen of one of the several states, in that the former is a special class of citizen created by Congress."

The "United States" is defined in Title 28 USC Sec. 3002(15)(A) as a "Federal corporation".

It is also a municipal corporation.

> **Municipal.** *In narrower, more common, sense, it means pertaining to a local governmental unit, commonly, a city or town or other governmental unit.* **In its broader sense, it means pertaining to the public or governmental**

> *affairs of a state or nation or of a people.* Black's Law Dictionary 6th Ed.

So the federal corporation United States, that pertains to the public affairs of a people, would be a municipal corporation. The federal government pertains to the affairs of its sovereign people.

> **Municipal corporation. <u>A body corporate consisting of the inhabitants</u>** *of a designated area* **<u>created by the legislature</u>** *with or without the consent of such inhabitants for governmental purposes . . .*
>
> *A municipal corporation has a dual character, the one public and the other private, and exercises corresponding twofold functions and duties -- one class consisting of those acts performed by it in the exercise of delegated sovereign powers for benefit of people generally, as arm of the state, enforcing general laws made in pursuance of general policy of the state, and the other consisting of acts done in exercise of power of the municipal*

> *corporation for its own benefit, or for the benefit of its citizens alone, or* **_citizens of the municipal corporation and its immediate locality._** Black's 6th Ed.

A municipal corporation is an artificial person, as shown above, and consists of the general inhabitants called citizens, and these artificial persons (citizens) were created by the legislature, not by God. A corporation can be a citizen itself, and that corporation can have its own citizens. A corporation also has it's own officers. When a corporation is dissolved, then the officers of that corporation no longer exist. A government has it's own citizens and employees. When that government is dissolved, then those citizens also cease to exist, since both officers and citizens of a corporation are both artificial persons.

> **Corporate citizen.** *Corporate status in the state of incorporation* . . . Black's 6th Ed.

A municipal corporation in its broader sense, such as the United States, consists of the inhabitants (U.S. citizens) of a designated area (federal United States). And a corporation can through its legislative branch create artificial persons, who are termed citizens of the municipal corporation. Can an artificial person create a flesh and blood natural man? Can the creator create a being superior to itself? Or can an artificial person only create (make) another artificial person?

I claim that when the municipal corporation United States, creates a citizen through legislative act, that citizen is then a corporate U.S. citizen. That corporate citizen's name is spelled in all capital letters, to indicate that it is an artificial person, as distinguished from a natural person whose name is spelled in upper and lower case letters. That corporate citizen is subject to its creator, the U.S. government, and is subject to its exclusive jurisdiction.

Constitution of the United States of America

14th Amendment. *Section 1. All **persons** born or **naturalized** in the United States and subject to the jurisdiction thereof, are citizens of the United States and of the State wherein they reside. No State shall make or enforce any law which shall abridge the privileges and immunities of citizens of the United States; nor shall any States deprive any person of life, liberty,* *or property, without due process of law; nor deny to any person within its jurisdiction the equal protection of the laws.*

A citizen of the United States is a corporate citizen, **with corporate status,** created by the corporation called United States, and is acting as their agent for the purpose of collecting revenue. This citizen has only privileges and immunities under the 14th Amendment. A natural person has inalienable rights, secured by the Constitution. A person with corporate status, would have corporate income.

COLLECTIVE ENTITY RULE

> **Braswell v.** United States 487 U.S. 99 (1988) *This doctrine - known as the **collective entity** rule- has a lengthy and distinguished pedigree.*

What is a "collective entity"? A collective entity is simply a corporate entity. Since the status of a U.S. citizen can be created by naturalization let's see what naturalization is, and determine if a U.S. citizen is part of a collective entity.

Naturalization. *The process by which a person acquires nationality **after birth** and becomes entitled to the **privileges of U.S. citizenship**. In the United States **collective** naturalization occurs when **designated groups** are **made** citizens by treaty (as Louisiana Purchase), or **by a law of Congress** (as in annexation of Texas and Hawaii).* Black's 6th Ed.

Person. *Scope and delineation of term necessary for determining to whom Fourteenth Amendment of Constitution affords protections since this Amendment expressly applies to "person".*

Let's review the definition of artificial person.

Artificial persons. *Persons created and devised by human laws for the purposes of society and government, as distinguished from natural persons.* *Corporations are examples of artificial persons.* Black's 6th Ed.

The 14th Amendment applies to "persons", and person in legal parlance means an artificial person, in distinction from a natural person. *"Collective" "naturalization occurs when designated groups"* (inhabitants) *"are **made** (created) citizens by a law of Congress"*. These artificial persons were *"created and devised by human laws* (14th Amendment U.S. citizen) *for the* (revenue) *purposes of society and government"*, and have their names spelled in all capital letters. These designated groups are "made" or created corporate citizens/employees and are distinguished from natural persons.

A natural person, with his name spelled in upper and lower case letters, has inalienable rights, and is NOT a corporate U.S. citizen. An artificial person, and corporate citizen of the United States, has his name spelled in all capital letters. A natural person cannot be an artificial person at the same time.

> The theme of the collective entity rule states:
>
> **Braswell v. United States 487 U.S. 99 (1988) quoting, United States v. White 322 U.S. 694 (1944)** *But individuals, when acting as representatives of a collective group, cannot be said to be exercising their*

> *personal rights and duties, nor be entitled to their purely personal privileges. Rather <u>they assume</u> the rights, duties and privileges of the artificial entity or association of which they are **agents** or officers and they are bound by its obligations.*

Under the collective entity rule, if John Joseph Smith contracted to be a representative or agent of the corporate citizen JOHN JOSEPH SMITH, then he would not be able to exercise his inalienable rights, which are his personal rights. John Joseph Smith (American Citizen) is contracting to be the agent of JOHN JOSEPH SMITH (U.S. citizen), thereby waiving his inalienable rights.

After the birth of John Joseph Smith, a new artificial person was created (JOHN JOSEPH SMITH), by the 14th Amendment, under the collective entity rule, and was naturalized as a corporate citizen of the United States. This did not destroy the natural person, but simply created a second separate legal entity, a legal fiction, artificial person. This legal fiction was created as an agent (U.S. citizen) of the corporate U.S. government to engage in commerce and collect revenue for the governments, federal, state, and local. You contracted to represent this artificial person, thereby waiving your inalienable rights.

A sovereign flesh and blood person is an American Citizen.

A corporate U.S. citizen is an artificial person and is a government agent/employee.

Birth Certificates are Federal Bank Notes

The American Bank Note Bldg. American Bank Note Company is a subsidiary of American Banknote Corporation and products range from currencies and credit cards to passports, driver's licenses, and birth certificates.

In the USA, citizens have never obtained their original Birth Certificates — what they possess is a copy. Furthermore, these 'copies' have a serial number on them, issued on special Bank Bond paper and authorized by "The American Bank Note Company". (More on this later).

The original birth or naturalization record for every U.S. Citizen is held with Washington, D.C. and the property and assets of every living U.S. Citizen is pledged as collateral for the National Debt.

Every citizen is given a number (*the red number on the Birth Certificate) and each live birth is reported to be valued at 650,000 to 750,000 Federal Reserve dollars in collateral from the Fed. Hence the saying "we are owned by the system".LITERALLY.

FACT: The government recognizes two distinct classes of citizens: a state Citizen and a federal citizen. Learn the difference now.

"There are hundreds of thousands of sovereigns in the United States of America but I am not one of them. The sovereigns own their land in "allodium." That is, the government does not have a financial interest in their land. Because of this they do not need to pay property tax (school tax, real estate tax). Only the powers granted to the federal government in the Constitution for the United States of America define the laws that they have to follow.

This is a very small subset of the laws most of us have to follow. Unless they accept benefits from or contract with the federal government, they do not have to pay Social Security tax, federal income tax, or resident individual state income tax.

They do not need to register their cars or get a driver's license unless they drive commercially. They will not have to get a Health Security Card. They can own any kind of gun without a license or permit. They do not have to use the same court system that normal people do. ~

*See below for information re: **State Citizenship (How to become a…)**

"Unbeknownst to most people, the class termed "US citizen" did not exist as a political status until 1866. It was a class and "political status" created for the newly freed slaves and did not apply to the people inhabiting the states of the union who were at that time state Citizens." ~ Mr. Richard James, McDonald, former law enforcement, California

Now do the math.

If indeed 317 million US citizens are worth an average of $700,000 in collateral for the US debt, that would mean the US is worth roughly 222 Trillion dollars.

Your birth certificate is really a *bank note*, which means you, the citizen are what is known in the *stock market as a commodity*.

DEFINITION of 'Commodity'

1. A basic good used in commerce that is interchangeable with other commodities of the same type. Commodities are most often used as inputs in the production of other goods or services. The quality of a given commodity may differ slightly, but it is essentially uniform across producers. When they are traded on an exchange, commodities must also meet specified minimum standards, also known as a basis grade.

2. Any good exchanged during commerce, which includes goods traded on a commodity exchange.

So if you didn't catch it the first time, I will repeat myself at the risk of being redundant. Us citizens are owned by The United States Federal reserve, a note in the stock exchange, being traded as a commodity.

The note is printed by The American Bank Note Company. Who are they?

Background on American Bank Note Company: The following was printed to the editor by the New York times.

AMERICAN BANK NOTE COMPANY, NEW-YORK, Saturday, Dec. 2, 1865. NEW YORK TIMES

"To the Editor of New-York Times:

The attention of this company has been drawn to a paragraph from the Washington Star of the 30th ult., giving an account of some examination made at the Treasury Department as to the evidence of the surreptitious impression of a genuine plate, used by the counterfeiter in printing the backs of the spurious one hundred dollar compound interest note, having been taken after or before the plates and dies prepared by the American Bank Note Company were delivered by that company to the Treasury Department.

This paragraph states this "investigation shows that the **counterfeits are made up from a** *plate surreptitiously obtained from this (the American Bank Note) Company."*

This statement is supported by a supposed demonstration, which to those familiar with the business will need no refutation, and which would amuse the counterfeiter, whoever he may be. And as no other reason, and no actual proof is pretended to support this imputation upon the security of plates and dies in the custody of the company, the paragraph might be left to every careful reader's own correction.

I beg, however, the favor of stating, through your paper, that this company is ready to submit to, and give every aid to, any examination into the matter which the Treasury Department may desire; and that "experts" or plain men, upon the most thorough scrutiny, will have no doubt that the surreptitious impression was made from the genuine plate in the hands of the government, and after it was changed from the condition in which it was delivered by this company. Very respectfully, your obedient servant,

~GEO. W. HATCH, President."

American Bank Note Company is a subsidiary of American Banknote Corporation and ABnote Group: http://abnote.com/

Today, following a variety of financial transformations, the American Banknote Corporation produces a wide variety of secure and official documents. With operations world wide its products range from currencies and credit cards to passports, driver's licenses, and *birth certificates*.

How does this work?

Why didn't you learn this in school? According to many sources, including an excerpt from researcher Brian Kelly,

"When the UNITED STATES declared bankruptcy, pledged all Americans as collateral against the national debt, and confiscated all gold, eliminating the means by which you could pay, it also assumed legal responsibility for providing a new way for you to pay, and it did that by providing what is known as the Exemption, an exemption from having to pay for anything. In practical terms, though, this meant giving each American something to pay with, and that \"something\" is your credit.

Your value to society was then and still is calculated using actuarial tables and at birth, bonds equal to this \"average value\" are created. I understand that this is currently between one and two million dollars. These bonds are collateralized by your birth certificate which becomes a negotiable instrument. The bonds are hypothecated, traded until their value is unlimited for all intents and purposes, and all that credit created is technically and rightfully yours.

In point of fact, you should be able to go into any store in America and buy anything and everything in sight, telling the clerk to charge it to your Exemption account, which is identified by a nine-digit number that you will recognize as your Social Security number without the dashes. It is your EIN, which stands for Exemption Identification Number."

The FEDERAL RESERVE BANK is not owned and controlled by the U.S. Government, rather it is owned and operated by International families. You are owned by foreigners bankers and your (physical) body is a collateral bond that has been issued on all your future earnings, your children's future earnings, etc. Were you taught this in school?

Why not?

If this is indeed the case, how do you change your current status?

The fact is, thousands of citizens have already changed their 'slavery' status by means of relinquishing the agreement and reverting to their Sovereign status (inalienable rights), the status you were born with such as *constitutional rights of life, liberty, and property which are not transferable and, thus, are termed inalienable.*

The Uniform Commercial Code (UCC) and the law of contracts make it difficult to conduct business in the USA. Now that you know your Birth certificate(registration of birth) is nothing more than a Contract with the government, what will you do to change this? Did they tell you you were signing a contract. Did you know that you didn't even have to register the birth?

Here are just some of the rights that you GAIN BACK as a Sovereign Citizen.

The first thing a Sovereign becomes is immune to law, I.E. statutory, civil and vehicle codes. You no longer are subject to those laws they just do not apply to you.

You gain the ability to discharge anything in the legal arena of commerce using the laws of that system against the perpetrators that are currently using those laws against you for their gain.

Becoming the Sovereign Citizen you were born to be, which is the master over the legal system rather than the servant you are now as a statutory citizen. (Note the Capitalization of the letter C) You were born a Sovereign but it only lasted a few hours or maybe a day at the most before you were illegally brought into the system by contract known as a birth certificate. That certificate made you a servant to the world we know as the UNITED STATES and the so called American way.

1. Discharging your debts by bonds.
2. Never having to pay a traffic ticket again if you so choose.
3. You cannot be sued in any court in this country.

Legally eliminate paying income taxes both federal and state. NOTE: The system will fight you on this to keep control over you even though they know it is legal for you to leave the system.

Get all the money you have ever paid into the system returned back to you with interest from the IRS. Again they will not willingly return your money.

stop paying any more into the IRS, you can legally stop the stealing at the source with your employer.

Duality! What's that?
Have you been told you have a TWIN somewhere in the world?
What's a TWIN?
Well let's start with duality..Duality-an instance of opposition or contrast between two concepts or two aspects of something;a dualism. Now lets look at TWIN-something containing or consisting of two matching or corresponding parts
TWIN Flames what's that?-A intense soul connection with someone thought to be a person's other half sometimes called a "mirror soul".
Okay! I'm about to lose you..Break down to me a STRAWMAN!..It would be my pleasure-A strawman is a form of argument and an informal fallacy of having the impression of refuting an argument whereas the real subject of the argument was not

addressed or refuted. But instead it was replaced with a false one. One who engages in this fallacy is said to be "attacking a strawman"
2. A person regarded as having no substance or integrity 3. Weak or imaginary opposition (such as an argument or adversary) set up to be easily confused. 4. A person set up to serve as cover for a usually questionable transaction.
Let's go back to Fallacy-A mistaken belief one based on unsound argument. 2. A failure in reasoning which renders an argument invalid. Jump to the definition of corresponding states-having or participating in the same relationship. 2. Analogous or equivalent in character form or function comparable. Define character-The aggregate of features and traits that form the individual nature of some person or thing. 3. Moral or ethical quality.

Let's stop right there to see if you're still with me. We discussed Duality, whats a TWIN, A TWIN Flame a STRAWMAN!(and I hope you really paid attention to the strawman definition). We discussed a Fallacy and also what the word corresponding means as well as character. Now there is a link to all these words (keep in mind)as I break down a little bit more for your reading pleasure what DUALITY means.

The DUALITY is what separates "TRUTH" into two parts. Two parts of the same whole, the

"PERCEIVED" relative truth and the "INHERENTLY" ABSOLUTE TRUTH. If something is perceived, the absolute truth cannot be understood. Absolute truth lies beyond perception because perception is only ONE filter that can be used to view something (it is merely one angle and not all angles).

The true significance of understanding the duality is the further understanding that nothing we perceive is set in stone. This means that old perceptions ascribed meaning, and other "TRUTHS" can be overturned and rewritten. We as beings of perceptions are free to change our perspectives and ascribe new relative values to things. We can overturn old traditions and ways of living and running society and install newer ones that we see fit. The duality makes us more humble when we come to understand that all distinctions are relative to something. To say we are "intelligent" is a relative statement but this relativity goes both way: in relation to ants we are more intelligent, but in relation to the rest of the the ever expanding universe we are likely not that intelligent(the possibility of more intelligent life in such a massive and mostly unexplained universe is extremely probably). Any perceived value is not an absolute truth but a relative one, a truth that we can empower or destroy at any time.

To say anything has value is to be on one side of the coin; one side of the duality. True value cannot be created because a true value would already exist inherently in the object. Relative values are created but a better word is "perceived" we perceive the value of something we don't really create a value. All perceived values are false in this sense because the other side of the coin cannot be perceived but merely acknowledged. Egarim

Let's define Perceive-1. Become aware or conscious of (something) come to realize or understand. 2. Interpret or look on (someone or something) in a particular way. Inherently-1. In a permanent, essential, or characteristic way. 2. Involved in the constitution of essential character of something. 3. Belonging by nature or habit. Essential- 1. Absolutely necessary and extremely important. Nature-1. Inevitable. 2. Viewed or existing independently and not in relation to other things not relative or comparative. Truth-1. Is the property of being in accord with the fact or reality. In everyday language, truth is typically ascribed to things that aim to represent reality or otherwise correspond to it such as beliefs, propositions and declarative sentences. Truth is usually held to be the opposite of falsehood. We goin define Substance- The real physical matter of which a person or thing consists and which has a tangible solid presence. Integrity-The practice of being honest and showing a consistent and uncompromising adherence to strong moral and ethical principles and values regarded as the honesty and truthfulness or accuracy of one's actions. One more word we are going to define is Adversary-One that contends with, opposes or resists an enemy or opponent,a clever.

Human Energy Fields and Auric Bodies

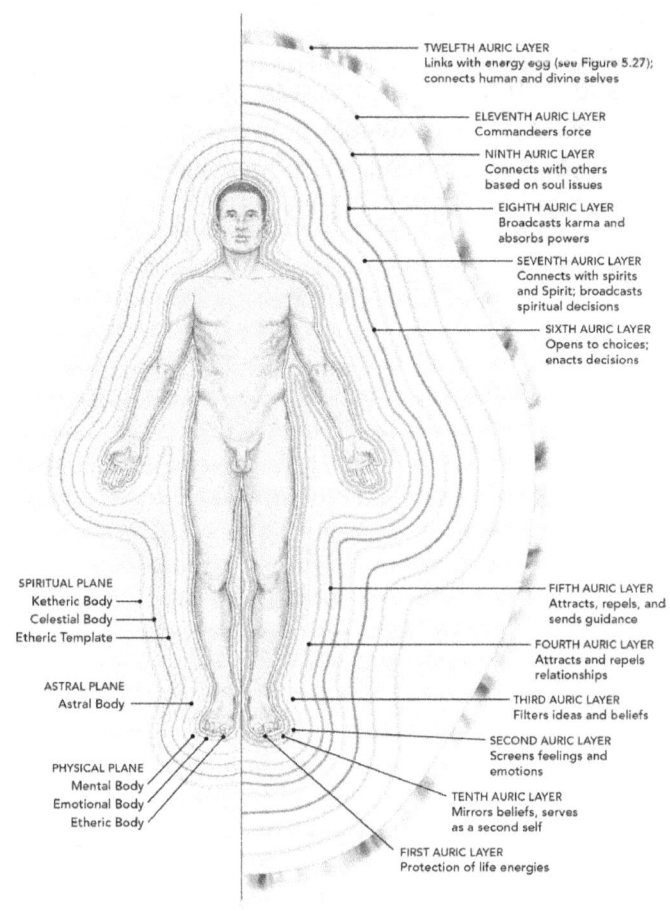

First Auric Layer-Protection of life energies

Second Auric Layer-Screens feelings and beliefs

Third Auric Layer-Filters Ideas and beliefs

Fourth Auric Layer-Attracts and repels relationship

Fifth Auric Layer-Attracts repels and sends guidance

Sixth Auric Layer-Open to choice enacts decisions

Seventh Auric Layer-Connects with spirits and spirit broadcast spiritual decisions

Eight Auric Layer-Broadcast Karma and Absorbs power

Ninth Auric Layer-Connects with others based on soul issues

Tenth Auric Layer-Mirrors beliefs serves as a second self

Eleventh Auric Layer-Commandeers force

Twelfth Auric Layer-Links with energy egg connects human and divine self

Spiritual Plane

Ketheric Body

Celestial Body

Etheric Template

Astral Plane

Astral Body

Physical Body

Mental Body

Emotional Body

Etheric Body

Electronic Harassment

In physics, **electromagnetic radiation (EM radiation** or **EMR)** refers to the waves (or their quanta, photons) of the electromagnetic field, propagating (radiating) through space, carrying electromagnetic radiant energy. It includes radio waves, microwaves, infrared, (visible) light, ultraviolet, X-rays, and gamma rays.

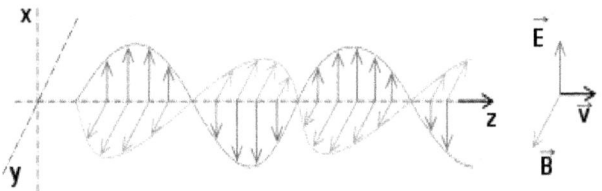

A linearly polarized sinusoidal electromagnetic wave, propagating in the direction **+z** through a homogeneous, isotropic, dissipationless medium, such as vacuum. The electric field (blue arrows) oscillates in the ±**x**-direction, and the orthogonal magnetic field (red arrows) oscillates in phase with the electric field, but in the ±**y**-direction.

Classically, electromagnetic radiation consists of **electromagnetic waves**, which are synchronized oscillations of electric and magnetic fields. In a vacuum, electromagnetic waves travel at the speed of light, commonly denoted c. In homogeneous, isotropic media, the oscillations of the two fields are perpendicular to each other and perpendicular to the direction of energy and wave propagation, forming a transverse wave. The wavefront of electromagnetic waves emitted from a point source (such as a light bulb) is a sphere. The position of an electromagnetic wave within the electromagnetic spectrum can be characterized by either its frequency of oscillation or its wavelength. Electromagnetic waves of different frequencies are called by different names since they have different sources and effects on matter. In order of increasing frequency and decreasing wavelength these are: radio waves, microwaves, infrared radiation, visible light, ultraviolet radiation, X-rays and gamma rays.

Electromagnetic waves are emitted by electrically charged particles undergoing acceleration, and these waves can subsequently interact with other charged particles, exerting force on them. EM waves carry energy, momentum and angular momentum away from their source particle and can impart those quantities to matter with which they interact. Electromagnetic radiation is associated with those EM waves that are free to propagate themselves ("radiate") without the continuing influence of the moving charges that produced them, because they have achieved sufficient distance from those charges. Thus, EMR is sometimes referred to as the far field. In this language, the near field refers to EM fields near the charges and current that directly produced them, specifically electromagnetic induction and electrostatic induction phenomena.

In quantum mechanics, an alternate way of viewing EMR is that it consists of photons, uncharged elementary particles with zero rest mass which are the quanta of the electromagnetic force, responsible for all electromagnetic interactions.Quantum electrodynamics is the theory of how EMR interacts with matter on an atomic level.Quantum effects provide additional sources of EMR, such as the transition of electrons to lower energy levels in an atom and black-body radiation. The energy of an individual photon is quantized and is greater for photons of higher frequency. This relationship is given by Planck's equation $E = hf$, where E is the energy per photon, f is the frequency of the photon, and h is Planck's constant. A single gamma ray photon, for example, might carry ~100,000 times the energy of a single photon of visible light.

The effects of EMR upon chemical compounds and biological organisms depend both upon the radiation's power and its frequency. EMR of visible or lower frequencies (i.e., visible light, infrared, microwaves, and radio waves) is called *non-ionizing radiation*, because its photons do not individually have enough energy to ionize atoms or molecules or break chemical bonds. The effects of these radiations on chemical systems and living tissue are caused primarily by heating effects from the combined energy transfer of many photons. In contrast, high frequency ultraviolet, X-rays and gamma rays are called *ionizing radiation*, since individual photons of such high frequency have enough energy to ionize molecules or break chemical bonds. These radiations have the ability to cause chemical reactions and damage living cells beyond that resulting from simple heating, and can be a health hazard.

Electronic harassment, electromagnetic torture, or **psychotronic torture** is a conspiracy theory that government agents make use of electromagnetic radiation (such as the microwave auditory effect), radar, and surveillance techniques to transmit sounds and thoughts into people's heads, affect people's bodies, and harass people. Individuals who claim to experience this call themselves "**targeted individuals**" ("**TI**s"). They claim they are victims of gang stalking and many have joined support and advocacy groups.

Multiple medical professionals have evaluated that these experiences are hallucinations; the result of delusional disorders or psychosis, the same sources from which arise religious delusions, accounts of alien abductions, and beliefs in visitations from dead relatives. It can be difficult to persuade people who experience them that their belief in an external influence is delusional.

The experiences of people who describe themselves as undergoing electronic

harassment using esoteric technology, and who call themselves "targeted individuals" ("T.I."), vary, but experiences often include hearing voices in their heads calling them by name, often mocking them or others around them, as well as physical sensations like burning. They have also described being under physical surveillance by one or more people. Many of these people act and function otherwise normally and included among them are people who are successful in their careers and lives otherwise, and who find these experiences confusing, upsetting, and sometimes shameful, but entirely real. They use news stories, military journals, and declassified national security documents to support their allegations that governments have developed technology that can send voices into people's heads and cause them to feel things. *The New York Times* estimated that there are more than 10,000 people who self-identify as targeted individuals.

Psychologist Lorraine Sheridan co-authored a study of gang-stalking in the *Journal of Forensic Psychiatry & Psychology*. According to Sheridan, "One has to think of the T.I. phenomenon in terms of people with paranoid symptoms who have hit upon the gang-stalking idea as an explanation of what is happening to them". Mental health professionals say that T.I.s can experience hallucinations and their explanations of being targeted or harassed arise from delusional disorders or psychosis. Yale psychiatry professor Ralph Hoffman states that people often ascribe voices in their heads to external sources such as government harassment, God, or dead relatives, and it can be difficult to persuade these individuals that their belief in an external influence is delusional.[ ] Other experts compare these stories to accounts of alien abductions.

Press accounts have documented individuals who apparently believed they were victims of electronic harassment, and in some cases persuaded courts to agree. In 2008, James Walbert went to court claiming that his former business associate had threatened him with "jolts of radiation" after a disagreement, and later claimed feeling symptoms such as electric shock sensations and hearing strange sounds in his ears. The court decided to issue an order banning "electronic means" to further harass Walbert.

Targeted surveillance (or targeted interception) is a form of surveillance, such as wiretapping, that is directed towards specific persons of interest, and is distinguishable from mass surveillance (or bulk interception). Both untargeted and targeted surveillance is routinely accused of treating innocent people as suspects in ways that are unfair, of violating human rights, international treaties and conventions as well as national laws, and of failing to pursue security effectively.

A 2014 report to the UN General Assembly by the United Nations' top official for counter-terrorism and human rights, condemned mass electronic surveillance as a clear violation of core privacy rights guaranteed by multiple treaties and conventions and makes a distinction between "targeted surveillance" - which "depend[s] upon the existence of prior suspicion of the targeted individual or organization" — and "mass surveillance", by which "states with high levels of Internet penetration can [...] gain access to the telephone and e-mail content of an effectively unlimited number of users and maintain an overview of Internet activity associated with particular websites".

The United Kingdom's House of Lords also distinguishes between these two broad types of surveillance:

- **Mass surveillance is also known as "passive" or "undirected" surveillance. [...] It is not targeted on any particular individual but gathers images and information for possible future use. CCTV and databases are examples of mass surveillance.**
- **Targeted surveillance is surveillance directed at particular individuals and can involve the use of specific powers by authorised public**

agencies. Targeted surveillance can be carried out overtly or covertly, and can involve human agents. Under the Regulation of Investigatory Powers Act 2000 (RIPA), targeted covert surveillance is "directed" if it is carried out for a specific investigation or operation. By comparison, if it is carried out on designated premises or on a vehicle, it is "intrusive" surveillance. Targeting methods include the interception of communications, the use of communications "traffic" data, visual surveillance devices, and devices that sense movement, objects or persons.

Only targeted interception of traffic and location data in order to combat serious crime, including terrorism, is justified, according to a decision by the European Court of Justice.